To an Old Mate

Old Mate! In the gusty old weather,
When our hopes and our troubles were new,
In the years spent in wearing out leather,
I found you unselfish and true —
I have gathered these verses together
For the sake of our friendship and you.

You may think for awhile, and with reason,
Though still with a kindly regret,
That I've left it full late in the season
To prove I remember you yet;
But you'll never judge me by their treason
Who profit by friends — and forget.

I remember, Old Man, I remember —
The tracks that we followed are clear —
The jovial last nights of December,
The solemn first days of the year,
Long tramps through the clearings and timber,
Short partings on platform and pier.

I can still feel the spirit that bore us,
And often the old stars will shine —
I remember the last spree in chorus
For the sake of that other Lang Syne,
When the tracks lay divided before us,
Your path through the future and mine.

Through the frost-wind that cut like whip-lashes,
Through the ever-blind haze of the drought —
And in fancy at times by the flashes
Of light in the darkness of doubt —
I have followed the tent poles and ashes
Of camps that we moved further out.

You will find in these pages a trace of
That side of our past which was bright,
And recognise sometimes the face of
A friend who has dropped out of sight —
I send them along in the place of
The letters I promised to write.

In the Days When the World was Wide

The world is narrow and ways are short, and our lives are dull and slow,
For little is new where the crowds resort, and less where the wanderers go;
Greater, or smaller, the same old things we see by the dull road-side —
And tired of all is the spirit that sings
of the days when the world was wide.

When the North was hale in the march of Time,
and the South and the West were new,
And the gorgeous East was a pantomime, as it seemed in our boyhood's view;
When Spain was first on the waves of change,
and proud in the ranks of pride,
And all was wonderful, new and strange in the days when the world was wide.

Then a man could fight if his heart were bold,
and win if his faith were true —
Were it love, or honour, or power, or gold, or all that our hearts pursue;
Could live to the world for the family name, or die for the family pride,
Could fly from sorrow, and wrong, and shame
in the days when the world was wide.

They sailed away in the ships that sailed ere science controlled the main,
When the strong, brave heart of a man prevailed
as 'twill never prevail again;
They knew not whither, nor much they cared —
let Fate or the winds decide —
The worst of the Great Unknown they dared
in the days when the world was wide.

They raised new stars on the silent sea that filled their hearts with awe;
They came to many a strange countree and marvellous sights they saw.
The villagers gaped at the tales they told,
and old eyes glistened with pride —
When barbarous cities were paved with gold
in the days when the world was wide.

'Twas honest metal and honest wood, in the days of the Outward Bound,
When men were gallant and ships were good — roaming the wide world round.
The gods could envy a leader then when 'Follow me, lads!' he cried —
They faced each other and fought like men
in the days when the world was wide.

They tried to live as a freeman should — they were happier men than we,
In the glorious days of wine and blood, when Liberty crossed the sea;
'Twas a comrade true or a foeman then, and a trusty sword well tried —
They faced each other and fought like men
in the days when the world was wide.

In the Days When the World Was Wide & Other Verses by Henry Lawson

Henry Archibald Hertzberg Lawson was born on the 17th June 1867 in a town on the Grenfell goldfields of New South Wales, Australia.

As a youth an ear infection had left him partially deaf and by fourteen he had lost his hearing completely.

He immersed himself in books to make up for the difficulties of a classroom education but later failed to gain entry to a University.

His first published poem was 'A Song of the Republic' in The Bulletin on 1st October 1887. This was quickly followed by other poems with one recognising him as "a youth whose poetic genius here speaks eloquently for itself."

In 1892, The Bulletin engaged him for an inland trip where he could write articles about the harsh realities of life in drought-stricken New South Wales. This resulted in his contributions to the Bulletin Debate and became the experience for a number of his stories in subsequent years. For Lawson this was an eye-opening period. His grim view of the outback was far removed from the romantic idyll of contemporary poetry and literature.

In 1896, Lawson married Bertha Bredt, Jr. but the marriage ended in June 1903. They had two children.

Despite this Lawson was finding his way in the literary world and achieving recognition. His most successful prose collection 'While the Billy Boils', was published in 1896. In it he virtually reinvented Australian realism.

His writing style of short, sharp sentences with honed and sparse descriptions created a personal writing style that defined Australians: dryly laconic, passionately egalitarian and deeply humane.

Sadly, for Lawson despite his growing recognition and fame he became withdrawn and unable to take part in the usual routines of life. His struggles with alcohol and mental health issues continued to drain him. His once prolific literary output began to decline. At times he was destitute mainly due, despite good sales and an enthusiastic audience, to ruinous publishing deals he had entered into.

Henry Archibald Hertzberg Lawson died, of cerebral hemorrhage, in Abbotsford, Sydney on 2nd September 1922.

Index of Contents

The good ship bound for the Southern seas when the beacon was Ballarat,
With a 'Ship ahoy!' on the freshening breeze,
'Where bound?' and 'What ship's that?' —
The emigrant train to New Mexico — the rush to the Lachlan Side —
Ah! faint is the echo of Westward Ho!
from the days when the world was wide.

South, East, and West in advance of Time — and, ay! in advance of Thought
Those brave men rose to a height sublime — and is it for this they fought?
And is it for this damned life we praise the god-like spirit that died
At Eureka Stockade in the Roaring Days
with the days when the world was wide?

We fight like women, and feel as much; the thoughts of our hearts we guard;
Where scarcely the scorn of a god could touch,
the sneer of a sneak hits hard;
The treacherous tongue and cowardly pen, the weapons of curs, decide —
They faced each other and fought like men
in the days when the world was wide.

Think of it all — of the life that is! Study your friends and foes!
Study the past! And answer this: 'Are these times better than those?'
The life-long quarrel, the paltry spite, the sting of your poisoned pride!
No matter who fell it were better to fight
as they did when the world was wide.

Boast as you will of your mateship now — crippled and mean and sly —
The lines of suspicion on friendship's brow
were traced since the days gone by.
There was room in the long, free lines of the van
to fight for it side by side —
There was beating-room for the heart of a man
in the days when the world was wide.

With its dull, brown days of a-shilling-an-hour
the dreary year drags round:
Is this the result of Old England's power?
— the bourne of the Outward Bound?
Is this the sequel of Westward Ho! — of the days of Whate'er Betide?
The heart of the rebel makes answer 'No!
We'll fight till the world grows wide!'

The world shall yet be a wider world — for the tokens are manifest;
East and North shall the wrongs be hurled that followed us South and West.
The march of Freedom is North by the Dawn! Follow, whate'er betide!
Sons of the Exiles, march! March on! March till the world grows wide!

Faces in the Street

They lie, the men who tell us in a loud decisive tone
That want is here a stranger, and that misery's unknown;
For where the nearest suburb and the city proper meet
My window-sill is level with the faces in the street —
Drifting past, drifting past,
To the beat of weary feet —
While I sorrow for the owners of those faces in the street.

And cause I have to sorrow, in a land so young and fair,
To see upon those faces stamped the marks of Want and Care;
I look in vain for traces of the fresh and fair and sweet
In sallow, sunken faces that are drifting through the street —
Drifting on, drifting on,
To the scrape of restless feet;
I can sorrow for the owners of the faces in the street.

In hours before the dawning dims the starlight in the sky
The wan and weary faces first begin to trickle by,
Increasing as the moments hurry on with morning feet,
Till like a pallid river flow the faces in the street —
Flowing in, flowing in,
To the beat of hurried feet —
Ah! I sorrow for the owners of those faces in the street.

The human river dwindles when 'tis past the hour of eight,
Its waves go flowing faster in the fear of being late;
But slowly drag the moments, whilst beneath the dust and heat
The city grinds the owners of the faces in the street —
Grinding body, grinding soul,
Yielding scarce enough to eat —
Oh! I sorrow for the owners of the faces in the street.

And then the only faces till the sun is sinking down
Are those of outside toilers and the idlers of the town,
Save here and there a face that seems a stranger in the street,
Tells of the city's unemployed upon his weary beat —
Drifting round, drifting round,
To the tread of listless feet —
Ah! My heart aches for the owner of that sad face in the street.

And when the hours on lagging feet have slowly dragged away,
And sickly yellow gaslights rise to mock the going day,
Then flowing past my window like a tide in its retreat,
Again I see the pallid stream of faces in the street —
Ebbing out, ebbing out,

To the drag of tired feet,
While my heart is aching dumbly for the faces in the street.

And now all blurred and smirched with vice the day's sad pages end,
For while the short 'large hours' toward the longer 'small hours' trend,
With smiles that mock the wearer, and with words that half entreat,
Delilah pleads for custom at the corner of the street —
Sinking down, sinking down,
Battered wreck by tempests beat —
A dreadful, thankless trade is hers, that Woman of the Street.

But, ah! to dreader things than these our fair young city comes,
For in its heart are growing thick the filthy dens and slums,
Where human forms shall rot away in sties for swine unmeet,
And ghostly faces shall be seen unfit for any street —
Rotting out, rotting out,
For the lack of air and meat —
In dens of vice and horror that are hidden from the street.

I wonder would the apathy of wealthy men endure
Were all their windows level with the faces of the Poor?
Ah! Mammon's slaves, your knees shall knock, your hearts in terror beat,
When God demands a reason for the sorrows of the street,
The wrong things and the bad things
And the sad things that we meet
In the filthy lane and alley, and the cruel, heartless street.

I left the dreadful corner where the steps are never still,
And sought another window overlooking gorge and hill;
But when the night came dreary with the driving rain and sleet,
They haunted me — the shadows of those faces in the street,
Flitting by, flitting by,
Flitting by with noiseless feet,
And with cheeks but little paler than the real ones in the street.

Once I cried: 'Oh, God Almighty! if Thy might doth still endure,
Now show me in a vision for the wrongs of Earth a cure.'
And, lo! with shops all shuttered I beheld a city's street,
And in the warning distance heard the tramp of many feet,
Coming near, coming near,
To a drum's dull distant beat,
And soon I saw the army that was marching down the street.

Then, like a swollen river that has broken bank and wall,
The human flood came pouring with the red flags over all,
And kindled eyes all blazing bright with revolution's heat,
And flashing swords reflecting rigid faces in the street.
Pouring on, pouring on,

To a drum's loud threatening beat,
And the war-hymns and the cheering of the people in the street.

And so it must be while the world goes rolling round its course,
The warning pen shall write in vain, the warning voice grow hoarse,
But not until a city feels Red Revolution's feet
Shall its sad people miss awhile the terrors of the street —
The dreadful everlasting strife
For scarcely clothes and meat
In that pent track of living death — the city's cruel street.

The Roaring Days

The night too quickly passes
And we are growing old,
So let us fill our glasses
And toast the Days of Gold;
When finds of wondrous treasure
Set all the South ablaze,
And you and I were faithful mates
All through the roaring days!

Then stately ships came sailing
From every harbour's mouth,
And sought the land of promise
That beaconed in the South;
Then southward streamed their streamers
And swelled their canvas full
To speed the wildest dreamers
E'er borne in vessel's hull.

Their shining Eldorado,
Beneath the southern skies,
Was day and night for ever
Before their eager eyes.
The brooding bush, awakened,
Was stirred in wild unrest,
And all the year a human stream
Went pouring to the West.

The rough bush roads re-echoed
The bar-room's noisy din,
When troops of stalwart horsemen
Dismounted at the inn.
And oft the hearty greetings
And hearty clasp of hands

Would tell of sudden meetings
Of friends from other lands;
When, puzzled long, the new-chum
Would recognise at last,
Behind a bronzed and bearded skin,
A comrade of the past.

And when the cheery camp-fire
Explored the bush with gleams,
The camping-grounds were crowded
With caravans of teams;
Then home the jests were driven,
And good old songs were sung,
And choruses were given
The strength of heart and lung.
Oh, they were lion-hearted
Who gave our country birth!
Oh, they were of the stoutest sons
From all the lands on earth!

Oft when the camps were dreaming,
And fires began to pale,
Through rugged ranges gleaming
Would come the Royal Mail.
Behind six foaming horses,
And lit by flashing lamps,
Old 'Cobb and Co.'s', in royal state,
Went dashing past the camps.

Oh, who would paint a goldfield,
And limn the picture right,
As we have often seen it
In early morning's light;
The yellow mounds of mullock
With spots of red and white,
The scattered quartz that glistened
Like diamonds in light;
The azure line of ridges,
The bush of darkest green,
The little homes of calico
That dotted all the scene.

I hear the fall of timber
From distant flats and fells,
The pealing of the anvils
As clear as little bells,
The rattle of the cradle,
The clack of windlass-boles,

The flutter of the crimson flags
Above the golden holes.

Ah, then our hearts were bolder,
And if Dame Fortune frowned
Our swags we'd lightly shoulder
And tramp to other ground.
But golden days are vanished,
And altered is the scene;
The diggings are deserted,
The camping-grounds are green;
The flaunting flag of progress
Is in the West unfurled,
The mighty bush with iron rails
Is tethered to the world.

'For'ard'

It is stuffy in the steerage where the second-classers sleep,
For there's near a hundred for'ard, and they're stowed away like sheep, —
They are trav'lers for the most part in a straight 'n' honest path;
But their linen's rather scanty, an' there isn't any bath —
Stowed away like ewes and wethers that is shore 'n' marked 'n' draft.
But the shearers of the shearers always seem to travel aft;
In the cushioned cabins, aft,
With saloons 'n' smoke-rooms, aft —
There is sheets 'n' best of tucker for the first-salooners, aft.

Our beef is just like scrapin's from the inside of a hide,
And the spuds were pulled too early, for they're mostly green inside;
But from somewhere back amidships there's a smell o' cookin' waft,
An' I'd give my earthly prospects for a real good tuck-out aft —
Ham an' eggs 'n' coffee, aft,
Say, cold fowl for luncheon, aft,
Juicy grills an' toast 'n' cutlets — tucker a-lor-frongsy, aft.

They feed our women sep'rate, an' they make a blessed fuss,
Just as if they couldn't trust 'em for to eat along with us!
Just because our hands are horny an' our hearts are rough with graft —
But the gentlemen and ladies always DINE together, aft —
With their ferns an' mirrors, aft,
With their flow'rs an' napkins, aft —
'I'll assist you to an orange' — 'Kindly pass the sugar', aft.

We are shabby, rough, 'n' dirty, an' our feelin's out of tune,
An' it's hard on fellers for'ard that was used to go saloon;

There's a broken swell among us — he is barracked, he is chaffed,
An' I wish at times, poor devil, for his own sake he was aft;
For they'd understand him, aft,
(He will miss the bath-rooms aft),
Spite of all there's no denyin' that there's finer feelin's aft.

Last night we watched the moonlight as it spread across the sea —
'It is hard to make a livin',' said the broken swell to me.
'There is ups an' downs,' I answered, an' a bitter laugh he laughed —
There were brighter days an' better when he always travelled aft —
With his rug an' gladstone, aft,
With his cap an' spyglass, aft —
A careless, rovin', gay young spark as always travelled aft.

There's a notice by the gangway, an' it seems to come amiss,
For it says that second-classers 'ain't allowed abaft o' this';
An' there ought to be a notice for the fellows from abaft —
But the smell an' dirt's a warnin' to the first-salooners, aft;
With their tooth and nail-brush, aft,
With their cuffs 'n' collars, aft —
Their cigars an' books an' papers, an' their cap-peaks fore-'n'-aft.

I want to breathe the mornin' breeze that blows against the boat,
For there's a swellin' in my heart — a tightness in my throat —
We are for'ard when there's trouble! We are for'ard when there's graft!
But the men who never battle always seem to travel aft;
With their dressin'-cases, aft,
With their swell pyjamas, aft —
Yes! the idle and the careless, they have ease an' comfort, aft.

I feel so low an' wretched, as I mooch about the deck,
That I'm ripe for jumpin' over — an' I wish there was a wreck!
We are driven to New Zealand to be shot out over there —
Scarce a shillin' in our pockets, nor a decent rag to wear,
With the everlastin' worry lest we don't get into graft —
There is little left to land for if you cannot travel aft;
No anxiety abaft,
They have stuff to land with, aft —
Oh, there's little left to land for if you cannot travel aft;

But it's grand at sea this mornin', an' Creation almost speaks,
Sailin' past the Bay of Islands with its pinnacles an' peaks,
With the sunny haze all round us an' the white-caps on the blue,
An' the orphan rocks an' breakers — Oh, it's glorious sailin' through!
To the south a distant steamer, to the west a coastin' craft,
An' we see the beauty for'ard, better than if we were aft;
Spite of op'ra-glasses, aft;
But, ah well, they're brothers aft —

Nature seems to draw us closer — bring us nearer fore-'n'-aft.

What's the use of bein' bitter? What's the use of gettin' mad?
What's the use of bein' narrer just because yer luck is bad?
What's the blessed use of frettin' like a child that wants the moon?
There is broken hearts an' trouble in the gilded first saloon!
We are used to bein' shabby — we have got no overdraft —
We can laugh at troubles for'ard that they couldn't laugh at aft;
Spite o' pride an' tone abaft
(Keepin' up appearance, aft)
There's anxiety an' worry in the breezy cabins aft.

But the curse o' class distinctions from our shoulders shall be hurled,
An' the influence of woman revolutionize the world;
There'll be higher education for the toilin' starvin' clown,
An' the rich an' educated shall be educated down;
An' we all will meet amidships on this stout old earthly craft,
An' there won't be any friction 'twixt the classes fore-'n'-aft.
We'll be brothers, fore-'n'-aft!
Yes, an' sisters, fore-'n'-aft!
When the people work together, and there ain't no fore-'n'-aft.

The Drover's Sweetheart

An hour before the sun goes down
Behind the ragged boughs,
I go across the little run
And bring the dusty cows;
And once I used to sit and rest
Beneath the fading dome,
For there was one that I loved best
Who'd bring the cattle home.

Our yard is fixed with double bails,
Round one the grass is green,
The bush is growing through the rails,
The spike is rusted in;
And 'twas from there his freckled face
Would turn and smile at me —
He'd milk a dozen in the race
While I was milking three.

I milk eleven cows myself
Where once I milked but four;
I set the dishes on the shelf
And close the dairy door;

And when the glaring sunlight fails
And the fire shines through the cracks,
I climb the broken stockyard rails
And watch the bridle-tracks.

He kissed me twice and once again
And rode across the hill,
The pint-pots and the hobble-chain
I hear them jingling still;
He'll come at night or not at all —
He left in dust and heat,
And when the soft, cool shadows fall
Is the best time to meet.

And he is coming back again,
He wrote to let me know,
The floods were in the Darling then —
It seems so long ago;
He'd come through miles of slush and mud,
And it was weary work,
The creeks were bankers, and the flood
Was forty miles round Bourke.

He said the floods had formed a block,
The plains could not be crossed,
And there was foot-rot in the flock
And hundreds had been lost;
The sheep were falling thick and fast
A hundred miles from town,
And when he reached the line at last
He trucked the remnant down.

And so he'll have to stand the cost;
His luck was always bad,
Instead of making more, he lost
The money that he had;
And how he'll manage, heaven knows
(My eyes are getting dim),
He says — he says — he don't — suppose
I'll want — to — marry — him.

As if I wouldn't take his hand
Without a golden glove —
Oh! Jack, you men won't understand
How much a girl can love.
I long to see his face once more —
Jack's dog! thank God, it's Jack! —
(I never thought I'd faint before)

He's coming — up — the track.

Out Back

The old year went, and the new returned, in the withering weeks of drought,
The cheque was spent that the shearer earned,
and the sheds were all cut out;
The publican's words were short and few,
and the publican's looks were black —
And the time had come, as the shearer knew, to carry his swag Out Back.

For time means tucker, and tramp you must,
where the scrubs and plains are wide,
With seldom a track that a man can trust, or a mountain peak to guide;
All day long in the dust and heat — when summer is on the track —
With stinted stomachs and blistered feet,
they carry their swags Out Back.

He tramped away from the shanty there, when the days were long and hot,
With never a soul to know or care if he died on the track or not.
The poor of the city have friends in woe, no matter how much they lack,
But only God and the swagmen know how a poor man fares Out Back.

He begged his way on the parched Paroo and the Warrego tracks once more,
And lived like a dog, as the swagmen do, till the Western stations shore;
But men were many, and sheds were full, for work in the town was slack —
The traveller never got hands in wool,
though he tramped for a year Out Back.

In stifling noons when his back was wrung
by its load, and the air seemed dead,
And the water warmed in the bag that hung to his aching arm like lead,
Or in times of flood, when plains were seas,
and the scrubs were cold and black,
He ploughed in mud to his trembling knees, and paid for his sins Out Back.

He blamed himself in the year 'Too Late' —
in the heaviest hours of life —
'Twas little he dreamed that a shearing-mate had care of his home and wife;
There are times when wrongs from your kindred come,
and treacherous tongues attack —
When a man is better away from home, and dead to the world, Out Back.

And dirty and careless and old he wore, as his lamp of hope grew dim;
He tramped for years till the swag he bore seemed part of himself to him.
As a bullock drags in the sandy ruts, he followed the dreary track,

With never a thought but to reach the huts when the sun went down Out Back.

It chanced one day, when the north wind blew
in his face like a furnace-breath,
He left the track for a tank he knew — 'twas a short-cut to his death;
For the bed of the tank was hard and dry, and crossed with many a crack,
And, oh! it's a terrible thing to die of thirst in the scrub Out Back.

A drover came, but the fringe of law was eastward many a mile;
He never reported the thing he saw, for it was not worth his while.
The tanks are full and the grass is high in the mulga off the track,
Where the bleaching bones of a white man lie
by his mouldering swag Out Back.

For time means tucker, and tramp they must,
where the plains and scrubs are wide,
With seldom a track that a man can trust, or a mountain peak to guide;
All day long in the flies and heat the men of the outside track
With stinted stomachs and blistered feet
must carry their swags Out Back.

The Free-Selector's Daughter

I met her on the Lachlan Side —
A darling girl I thought her,
And ere I left I swore I'd win
The free-selector's daughter.

I milked her father's cows a month,
I brought the wood and water,
I mended all the broken fence,
Before I won the daughter.

I listened to her father's yarns,
I did just what I 'oughter',
And what you'll have to do to win
A free-selector's daughter.

I broke my pipe and burnt my twist,
And washed my mouth with water;
I had a shave before I kissed
The free-selector's daughter.

Then, rising in the frosty morn,
I brought the cows for Mary,
And when I'd milked a bucketful

I took it to the dairy.

I poured the milk into the dish
While Mary held the strainer,
I summoned heart to speak my wish,
And, oh! her blush grew plainer.

I told her I must leave the place,
I said that I would miss her;
At first she turned away her face,
And then she let me kiss her.

I put the bucket on the ground,
And in my arms I caught her:
I'd give the world to hold again
That free-selector's daughter!

'Sez You'

When the heavy sand is yielding backward from your blistered feet,
And across the distant timber you can SEE the flowing heat;
When your head is hot and aching, and the shadeless plain is wide,
And it's fifteen miles to water in the scrub the other side —
Don't give up, don't be down-hearted, to a man's strong heart be true!
Take the air in through your nostrils, set your lips and see it through —
For it can't go on for ever, and — 'I'll have my day!' says you.

When you're camping in the mulga, and the rain is falling slow,
While you nurse your rheumatism 'neath a patch of calico;
Short of tucker or tobacco, short of sugar or of tea,
And the scrubs are dark and dismal, and the plains are like a sea;
Don't give up and be down-hearted — to the soul of man be true!
Grin! if you've a mate to grin for, grin and jest and don't look blue;
For it can't go on for ever, and — 'I'll rise some day,' says you.

When you've tramped the Sydney pavements till you've counted all the flags,
And your flapping boot-soles trip you, and your clothes are mostly rags,
When you're called a city loafer, shunned, abused, moved on, despised —
Fifty hungry beggars after every job that's advertised —
Don't be beaten! Hold your head up! To your wretched self be true;
Set your pride to fight your hunger! Be a MAN in all you do!
For it cannot last for ever — 'I will rise again!' says you.

When you're dossing out in winter, in the darkness and the rain,
Crouching, cramped, and cold and hungry 'neath a seat in The Domain,
And a cloaked policeman stirs you with that mighty foot of his —

'Phwat d'ye mane? Phwat's this?
Who are ye? Come, move on — git out av this!'
Don't get mad; 'twere only foolish; there is nought that you can do,
Save to mark his beat and time him — find another hole or two;
But it can't go on for ever — 'I'll have money yet!' says you.

Bother not about the morrow, for sufficient to the day
Is the evil (rather more so). Put your trust in God and pray!
Study well the ant, thou sluggard. Blessed are the meek and low.
Ponder calmly on the lilies — how they idle, how they grow.
A man's a man! Obey your masters! Do not blame the proud and fat,
For the poor are always with them, and they cannot alter that.
Lay your treasures up in Heaven — cling to life and see it through!
For it cannot last for ever — 'I shall die some day,' says you.

Andy's Gone With Cattle

Our Andy's gone to battle now
'Gainst Drought, the red marauder;
Our Andy's gone with cattle now
Across the Queensland border.

He's left us in dejection now;
Our hearts with him are roving.
It's dull on this selection now,
Since Andy went a-droving.

Who now shall wear the cheerful face
In times when things are slackest?
And who shall whistle round the place
When Fortune frowns her blackest?

Oh, who shall cheek the squatter now
When he comes round us snarling?
His tongue is growing hotter now
Since Andy cross'd the Darling.

The gates are out of order now,
In storms the 'riders' rattle;
For far across the border now
Our Andy's gone with cattle.

Poor Aunty's looking thin and white;
And Uncle's cross with worry;
And poor old Blucher howls all night
Since Andy left Macquarie.

Oh, may the showers in torrents fall,
And all the tanks run over;
And may the grass grow green and tall
In pathways of the drover;

And may good angels send the rain
On desert stretches sandy;
And when the summer comes again
God grant 'twill bring us Andy.

Jack Dunn of Nevertire

It chanced upon the very day we'd got the shearing done,
A buggy brought a stranger to the West-o'-Sunday Run;
He had a round and jolly face, and he was sleek and stout,
He drove right up between the huts and called the super out.
We chaps were smoking after tea, and heard the swell enquire
For one as travelled by the name of 'Dunn of Nevertire'.
Jack Dunn of Nevertire,
Poor Dunn of Nevertire;
There wasn't one of us but knew Jack Dunn of Nevertire.

'Jack Dunn of Nevertire,' he said; 'I was a mate of his;
And now it's twenty years since I set eyes upon his phiz.
There is no whiter man than Jack — no straighter south the line,
There is no hand in all the land I'd sooner grip in mine;
To help a mate in trouble Jack would go through flood and fire.
Great Scott! and don't you know the name of Dunn of Nevertire?
Big Dunn of Nevertire,
Long Jack from Nevertire;
He stuck to me through thick and thin, Jack Dunn of Nevertire.

'I did a wild and foolish thing while Jack and I were mates,
And I disgraced my guv'nor's name, an' wished to try the States.
My lamps were turned to Yankee Land, for I'd some people there,
And I was right when someone sent the money for my fare;
I thought 'twas Dad until I took the trouble to enquire,
And found that he who sent the stuff was Dunn of Nevertire,
Jack Dunn of Nevertire,
Soft Dunn of Nevertire;
He'd won some money on a race — Jack Dunn of Nevertire.

'Now I've returned, by Liverpool, a swell of Yankee brand,
To reckon, guess, and kalkilate, 'n' wake my native land;
There is no better land, I swear, in all the wide world round —

I smelt the bush a month before we touched King George's Sound!
And now I've come to settle down, the top of my desire
Is just to meet a mate o' mine called 'Dunn of Nevertire'.
Was raised at Nevertire —
The town of Nevertire;
He humped his bluey by the name of 'Dunn of Nevertire'.

'I've heard he's poor, and if he is, a proud old fool is he;
But, spite of that, I'll find a way to fix the old gum-tree.
I've bought a station in the North — the best that could be had;
I want a man to pick the stock — I want a super bad;
I want no bully-brute to boss — no crawling, sneaking liar —
My station super's name shall be 'Jack Dunn of Nevertire'!
Straight Dunn of Nevertire,
Old Dunn of Nevertire;
I guess he's known up Queensland way — Jack Dunn of Nevertire.'

The super said, while to his face a strange expression came:
'I THINK I've seen the man you want, I THINK I know the name;
Had he a jolly kind of face, a free and careless way,
Gray eyes that always seem'd to smile, and hair just turning gray —
Clean-shaved, except a light moustache, long-limbed, an' tough as wire?'
'THAT'S HIM! THAT'S DUNN!' the stranger roared, 'Jack Dunn of Nevertire!
John Dunn of Nevertire,
Jack D. from Nevertire,
They said I'd find him here, the cuss! — Jack Dunn of Nevertire.

'I'd know his walk,' the stranger cried, 'though sobered, I'll allow.'
'I doubt it much,' the boss replied, 'he don't walk that way now.'
'Perhaps he don't!' the stranger said, 'for years were hard on Jack;
But, if he were a mile away, I swear I'd know his back.'
'I doubt it much,' the super said, and sadly puffed his briar,
'I guess he wears a pair of wings — Jack Dunn of Nevertire;
Jack Dunn of Nevertire,
Brave Dunn of Nevertire,
He caught a fever nursing me, Jack Dunn of Nevertire.'

We took the stranger round to where a gum-tree stood alone,
And in the grass beside the trunk he saw a granite stone;
The names of Dunn and Nevertire were plainly written there —
'I'm all broke up,' the stranger said, in sorrow and despair,
'I guess he has a wider run, the man that I require;
He's got a river-frontage now, Jack Dunn of Nevertire;
Straight Dunn of Nevertire,
White Jack from Nevertire,
I guess Saint Peter knew the name of 'Dunn of Nevertire'.'

Trooper Campbell

One day old Trooper Campbell
Rode out to Blackman's Run,
His cap-peak and his sabre
Were glancing in the sun.
'Twas New Year's Eve, and slowly
Across the ridges low
The sad Old Year was drifting
To where the old years go.

The trooper's mind was reading
The love-page of his life —
His love for Mary Wylie
Ere she was Blackman's wife;
He sorrowed for the sorrows
Of the heart a rival won,
For he knew that there was trouble
Out there on Blackman's Run.

The sapling shades had lengthened,
The summer day was late,
When Blackman met the trooper
Beyond the homestead gate.
And if the hand of trouble
Can leave a lasting trace,
The lines of care had come to stay
On poor old Blackman's face.

'Not good day, Trooper Campbell,
It's a bad, bad day for me —
You are of all the men on earth
The one I wished to see.
The great black clouds of trouble
Above our homestead hang;
That wild and reckless boy of mine
Has joined M'Durmer's gang.

'Oh! save him, save him, Campbell!
I beg in friendship's name!
For if they take and hang him,
The wife would die of shame.
Could Mary or her sisters
Hold up their heads again,
And face a woman's malice
Or claim the love of men?

'And if he does a murder
'Twere better we were dead.
Don't take him, Trooper Campbell,
If a price be on his head;
But shoot him! shoot him, Campbell,
When you meet him face to face,
And save him from the gallows,
And us from that disgrace.'

'Now, Tom,' cried Trooper Campbell,
'You know your words are wild.
Though he is wild and reckless,
Yet still he is your child;
So bear up in your trouble,
And meet it like a man,
And tell the wife and daughters
I'll save him if I can.'

The sad Australian sunset
Had faded from the west;
But night brings darker shadows
To hearts that cannot rest;
And Blackman's wife sat rocking
And moaning in her chair.
'I cannot bear disgrace,' she moaned;
'Disgrace I cannot bear.

'In hardship and in trouble
I struggled year by year
To make my children better
Than other children here.
And if my son's a felon
How can I show my face?
I cannot bear disgrace; my God,
I cannot bear disgrace!

'Ah, God in Heaven pardon!
I'm selfish in my woe —
My boy is better-hearted
Than many that I know.
And I will face the world's disgrace,
And, till his mother's dead,
My foolish child shall find a place
To lay his outlawed head.'

With a sad heart Trooper Campbell
Rode back from Blackman's Run,
Nor noticed aught about him

Till thirteen miles were done;
When, close beside a cutting,
He heard the click of locks,
And saw the rifle muzzles
Were on him from the rocks.

But suddenly a youth rode out,
And, close by Campbell's side:
'Don't fire! don't fire, in heaven's name!
It's Campbell, boys!' he cried.
Then one by one in silence
The levelled rifles fell,
For who'd shoot Trooper Campbell
Of those who knew him well?

Oh, bravely sat old Campbell,
No sign of fear showed he.
He slowly drew his carbine;
It rested by his knee.
The outlaws' guns were lifted,
But none the silence broke,
Till steadfastly and firmly
Old Trooper Campbell spoke.

'That boy that you would ruin
Goes home with me, my men;
Or some of us shall never
Ride through the Gap again.
You know old Trooper Campbell,
And have you ever heard
That bluff or lead could turn him,
That e'er he broke his word?

'That reckless lad is playing
A heartless villain's part;
He knows that he is breaking
His poor old mother's heart.
He'll bring a curse upon himself;
But 'tis not that alone,
He'll bring dishonour to a name
That I'D be proud to own.

'I speak to you, M'Durmer, —
If your heart's not hardened quite,
And if you'd seen the trouble
At Blackman's home this night,
You'd help me now, M'Durmer —
I speak as man to man —

I swore to save that foolish lad,
And I'll save him if I can.'

'Oh, take him!' said M'Durmer,
'He's got a horse to ride.'
The youngster thought a moment,
Then rode to Campbell's side —
'Good-bye!' the outlaws shouted,
As up the range they sped.
'A Merry New Year, Campbell,'
Was all M'Durmer said.

Then fast along the ridges
Two bushmen rode a race,
And the moonlight lent a glory
To Trooper Campbell's face.
And ere the new year's dawning
They reached the home at last;
And this is but a story
Of trouble that is past!

The Sliprails and the Spur

The colours of the setting sun
Withdrew across the Western land —
He raised the sliprails, one by one,
And shot them home with trembling hand;
Her brown hands clung — her face grew pale —
Ah! quivering chin and eyes that brim! —
One quick, fierce kiss across the rail,
And, 'Good-bye, Mary!' 'Good-bye, Jim!'

Oh, he rides hard to race the pain
Who rides from love, who rides from home;
But he rides slowly home again,
Whose heart has learnt to love and roam.

A hand upon the horse's mane,
And one foot in the stirrup set,
And, stooping back to kiss again,
With 'Good-bye, Mary! don't you fret!
When I come back' — he laughed for her —
'We do not know how soon 'twill be;
I'll whistle as I round the spur —
You let the sliprails down for me.'

She gasped for sudden loss of hope,
As, with a backward wave to her,
He cantered down the grassy slope
And swiftly round the dark'ning spur.
Black-pencilled panels standing high,
And darkness fading into stars,
And blurring fast against the sky,
A faint white form beside the bars.

And often at the set of sun,
In winter bleak and summer brown,
She'd steal across the little run,
And shyly let the sliprails down.
And listen there when darkness shut
The nearer spur in silence deep;
And when they called her from the hut
Steal home and cry herself to sleep.

(Some editions have four more lines)

And he rides hard to dull the pain
Who rides from one that loves him best;
And he rides slowly back again,
Whose restless heart must rove for rest.

Past Carin'

Now up and down the siding brown
The great black crows are flyin',
And down below the spur, I know,
Another 'milker's' dyin';
The crops have withered from the ground,
The tank's clay bed is glarin',
But from my heart no tear nor sound,
For I have gone past carin' —
Past worryin' or carin',
Past feelin' aught or carin';
But from my heart no tear nor sound,
For I have gone past carin'.

Through Death and Trouble, turn about,
Through hopeless desolation,
Through flood and fever, fire and drought,
And slavery and starvation;
Through childbirth, sickness, hurt, and blight,
And nervousness an' scarin',

Through bein' left alone at night,
I've got to be past carin'.
Past botherin' or carin',
Past feelin' and past carin';
Through city cheats and neighbours' spite,
I've come to be past carin'.

Our first child took, in days like these,
A cruel week in dyin',
All day upon her father's knees,
Or on my poor breast lyin';
The tears we shed — the prayers we said
Were awful, wild — despairin'!
I've pulled three through, and buried two
Since then — and I'm past carin'.
I've grown to be past carin',
Past worryin' and wearin';
I've pulled three through and buried two
Since then, and I'm past carin'.

'Twas ten years first, then came the worst,
All for a dusty clearin',
I thought, I thought my heart would burst
When first my man went shearin';
He's drovin' in the great North-west,
I don't know how he's farin';
For I, the one that loved him best,
Have grown to be past carin'.
I've grown to be past carin'
Past lookin' for or carin';
The girl that waited long ago,
Has lived to be past carin'.

My eyes are dry, I cannot cry,
I've got no heart for breakin',
But where it was in days gone by,
A dull and empty achin'.
My last boy ran away from me,
I know my temper's wearin',
But now I only wish to be
Beyond all signs of carin'.
Past wearyin' or carin',
Past feelin' and despairin';
And now I only wish to be
Beyond all signs of carin'.

The Glass on the Bar

Three bushmen one morning rode up to an inn,
And one of them called for the drinks with a grin;
They'd only returned from a trip to the North,
And, eager to greet them, the landlord came forth.
He absently poured out a glass of Three Star.
And set down that drink with the rest on the bar.

'There, that is for Harry,' he said, 'and it's queer,
'Tis the very same glass that he drank from last year;
His name's on the glass, you can read it like print,
He scratched it himself with an old piece of flint;
I remember his drink — it was always Three Star' —
And the landlord looked out through the door of the bar.

He looked at the horses, and counted but three:
'You were always together — where's Harry?' cried he.
Oh, sadly they looked at the glass as they said,
'You may put it away, for our old mate is dead;'
But one, gazing out o'er the ridges afar,
Said, 'We owe him a shout — leave the glass on the bar.'

They thought of the far-away grave on the plain,
They thought of the comrade who came not again,
They lifted their glasses, and sadly they said:
'We drink to the name of the mate who is dead.'
And the sunlight streamed in, and a light like a star
Seemed to glow in the depth of the glass on the bar.

And still in that shanty a tumbler is seen,
It stands by the clock, ever polished and clean;
And often the strangers will read as they pass
The name of a bushman engraved on the glass;
And though on the shelf but a dozen there are,
That glass never stands with the rest on the bar.

The Shanty on the Rise

When the caravans of wool-teams climbed the ranges from the West,
On a spur among the mountains stood 'The Bullock-drivers' Rest';
It was built of bark and saplings, and was rather rough inside,
But 'twas good enough for bushmen in the careless days that died —
Just a quiet little shanty kept by 'Something-in-Disguise',
As the bushmen called the landlord of the Shanty on the Rise.

City swells who 'do the Royal' would have called the Shanty low,
But 'twas better far and purer than some toney pubs I know;
For the patrons of the Shanty had the principles of men,
And the spieler, if he struck it, wasn't welcome there again.
You could smoke and drink in quiet, yarn, or else soliloquise,
With a decent lot of fellows in the Shanty on the Rise.

'Twas the bullock-driver's haven when his team was on the road,
And the waggon-wheels were groaning as they ploughed beneath the load;
And I mind how weary teamsters struggled on while it was light,
Just to camp within a cooey of the Shanty for the night;
And I think the very bullocks raised their heads and fixed their eyes
On the candle in the window of the Shanty on the Rise.

And the bullock-bells were clanking from the marshes on the flats
As we hurried to the Shanty, where we hung our dripping hats;
And we took a drop of something that was brought at our desire,
As we stood with steaming moleskins in the kitchen by the fire.
Oh! it roared upon a fireplace of the good, old-fashioned size,
When the rain came down the chimney of the Shanty on the Rise.

They got up a Christmas party in the Shanty long ago,
While I camped with Jimmy Nowlett on the riverbank below;
Poor old Jim was in his glory — they'd elected him M.C.,
For there wasn't such another raving lunatic as he.
'Mr. Nowlett, Mr. Swaller!' shouted Something-in-Disguise,
As we walked into the parlour of the Shanty on the Rise.

There is little real pleasure in the city where I am —
There's a swarry round the corner with its mockery and sham;
But a fellow can be happy when around the room he whirls
In a party up the country with the jolly country girls.
Why, at times I almost fancied I was dancing on the skies,
When I danced with Mary Carey in the Shanty on the Rise.

Jimmy came to me and whispered, and I muttered, 'Go along!'
But he shouted, 'Mr. Swaller will oblige us with a song!'
And at first I said I wouldn't, and I shammed a little too,
Till the girls began to whisper, 'Mr. Swallow, now, ah, DO!'
So I sang a song of something 'bout the love that never dies,
And the chorus shook the rafters of the Shanty on the Rise.

Jimmy burst his concertina, and the bullock-drivers went
For the corpse of Joe the Fiddler, who was sleeping in his tent;
Joe was tired and had lumbago, and he wouldn't come, he said,
But the case was very urgent, so they pulled him out of bed;
And they fetched him, for the bushmen knew that Something-in-Disguise
Had a cure for Joe's lumbago in the Shanty on the Rise.

Jim and I were rather quiet while escorting Mary home,
'Neath the stars that hung in clusters, near and distant, from the dome;
And we walked so very silent — being lost in reverie —
That we heard the settlers'-matches rustle softly on the tree;
And I wondered who would win her when she said her sweet good-byes —
But she died at one-and-twenty, and was buried on the Rise.

I suppose the Shanty vanished from the ranges long ago,
And the girls are mostly married to the chaps I used to know;
My old chums are in the distance — some have crossed the border-line,
But in fancy still their glasses chink against the rim of mine.
And, upon the very centre of the greenest spot that lies
In my fondest recollection, stands the Shanty on the Rise.

The Vagabond

White handkerchiefs wave from the short black pier
As we glide to the grand old sea —
But the song of my heart is for none to hear
If one of them waves for me.
A roving, roaming life is mine,
Ever by field or flood —
For not far back in my father's line
Was a dash of the Gipsy blood.

Flax and tussock and fern,
Gum and mulga and sand,
Reef and palm — but my fancies turn
Ever away from land;
Strange wild cities in ancient state,
Range and river and tree,
Snow and ice. But my star of fate
Is ever across the sea.

A god-like ride on a thundering sea,
When all but the stars are blind —
A desperate race from Eternity
With a gale-and-a-half behind.
A jovial spree in the cabin at night,
A song on the rolling deck,
A lark ashore with the ships in sight,
Till — a wreck goes down with a wreck.

A smoke and a yarn on the deck by day,
When life is a waking dream,

And care and trouble so far away
That out of your life they seem.
A roving spirit in sympathy,
Who has travelled the whole world o'er —
My heart forgets, in a week at sea,
The trouble of years on shore.

A rolling stone! — 'tis a saw for slaves —
Philosophy false as old —
Wear out or break 'neath the feet of knaves,
Or rot in your bed of mould!
But I'D rather trust to the darkest skies
And the wildest seas that roar,
Or die, where the stars of Nations rise,
In the stormy clouds of war.

Cleave to your country, home, and friends,
Die in a sordid strife —
You can count your friends on your finger ends
In the critical hours of life.
Sacrifice all for the family's sake,
Bow to their selfish rule!
Slave till your big soft heart they break —
The heart of the family fool.

Domestic quarrels, and family spite,
And your Native Land may be
Controlled by custom, but, come what might,
The rest of the world for me.
I'd sail with money, or sail without! —
If your love be forced from home,
And you dare enough, and your heart be stout,
The world is your own to roam.

I've never a love that can sting my pride,
Nor a friend to prove untrue;
For I leave my love ere the turning tide,
And my friends are all too new.
The curse of the Powers on a peace like ours,
With its greed and its treachery —
A stranger's hand, and a stranger land,
And the rest of the world for me!

But why be bitter? The world is cold
To one with a frozen heart;
New friends are often so like the old,
They seem of the past a part —
As a better part of the past appears,

When enemies, parted long,
Are come together in kinder years,
With their better nature strong.

I had a friend, ere my first ship sailed,
A friend that I never deserved —
For the selfish strain in my blood prevailed
As soon as my turn was served.
And the memory haunts my heart with shame —
Or, rather, the pride that's there;
In different guises, but soul the same,
I meet him everywhere.

I had a chum. When the times were tight
We starved in Australian scrubs;
We froze together in parks at night,
And laughed together in pubs.
And I often hear a laugh like his
From a sense of humour keen,
And catch a glimpse in a passing phiz
Of his broad, good-humoured grin.

And I had a love — 'twas a love to prize —
But I never went back again . . .
I have seen the light of her kind brown eyes
In many a face since then.

The sailors say 'twill be rough to-night,
As they fasten the hatches down,
The south is black, and the bar is white,
And the drifting smoke is brown.
The gold has gone from the western haze,
The sea-birds circle and swarm —
But we shall have plenty of sunny days,
And little enough of storm.

The hill is hiding the short black pier,
As the last white signal's seen;
The points run in, and the houses veer,
And the great bluff stands between.
So darkness swallows each far white speck
On many a wharf and quay.
The night comes down on a restless deck, —
Grim cliffs — and — The Open Sea!

Sweeney

It was somewhere in September, and the sun was going down,
When I came, in search of 'copy', to a Darling-River town;
'Come-and-have-a-drink' we'll call it — 'tis a fitting name, I think —
And 'twas raining, for a wonder, up at Come-and-have-a-drink.

'Neath the public-house verandah I was resting on a bunk
When a stranger rose before me, and he said that he was drunk;
He apologised for speaking; there was no offence, he swore;
But he somehow seemed to fancy that he'd seen my face before.

'No erfence,' he said. I told him that he needn't mention it,
For I might have met him somewhere; I had travelled round a bit,
And I knew a lot of fellows in the bush and in the streets —
But a fellow can't remember all the fellows that he meets.

Very old and thin and dirty were the garments that he wore,
Just a shirt and pair of trousers, and a boot, and nothing more;
He was wringing-wet, and really in a sad and sinful plight,
And his hat was in his left hand, and a bottle in his right.

His brow was broad and roomy, but its lines were somewhat harsh,
And a sensual mouth was hidden by a drooping, fair moustache;
(His hairy chest was open to what poets call the 'wined',
And I would have bet a thousand that his pants were gone behind).

He agreed: 'Yer can't remember all the chaps yer chance to meet,'
And he said his name was Sweeney — people lived in Sussex-street.
He was campin' in a stable, but he swore that he was right,
'Only for the blanky horses walkin' over him all night.'

He'd apparently been fighting, for his face was black-and-blue,
And he looked as though the horses had been treading on him, too;
But an honest, genial twinkle in the eye that wasn't hurt
Seemed to hint of something better, spite of drink and rags and dirt.

It appeared that he mistook me for a long-lost mate of his —
One of whom I was the image, both in figure and in phiz —
(He'd have had a letter from him if the chap were living still,
For they'd carried swags together from the Gulf to Broken Hill.)

Sweeney yarned awhile and hinted that his folks were doing well,
And he told me that his father kept the Southern Cross Hotel;
And I wondered if his absence was regarded as a loss
When he left the elder Sweeney — landlord of the Southern Cross.

He was born in Parramatta, and he said, with humour grim,
That he'd like to see the city ere the liquor finished him,

But he couldn't raise the money. He was damned if he could think
What the Government was doing. Here he offered me a drink.

I declined — 'TWAS self-denial — and I lectured him on booze,
Using all the hackneyed arguments that preachers mostly use;
Things I'd heard in temperance lectures (I was young and rather green),
And I ended by referring to the man he might have been.

Then a wise expression struggled with the bruises on his face,
Though his argument had scarcely any bearing on the case:
'What's the good o' keepin' sober? Fellers rise and fellers fall;
What I might have been and wasn't doesn't trouble me at all.'

But he couldn't stay to argue, for his beer was nearly gone.
He was glad, he said, to meet me, and he'd see me later on;
He guessed he'd have to go and get his bottle filled again,
And he gave a lurch and vanished in the darkness and the rain.

And of afternoons in cities, when the rain is on the land,
Visions come to me of Sweeney with his bottle in his hand,
With the stormy night behind him, and the pub verandah-post —
And I wonder why he haunts me more than any other ghost.

Still I see the shearers drinking at the township in the scrub,
And the army praying nightly at the door of every pub,
And the girls who flirt and giggle with the bushmen from the west —
But the memory of Sweeney overshadows all the rest.

Well, perhaps, it isn't funny; there were links between us two —
He had memories of cities, he had been a jackeroo;
And, perhaps, his face forewarned me of a face that I might see
From a bitter cup reflected in the wretched days to be.

I suppose he's tramping somewhere where the bushmen carry swags,
Cadging round the wretched stations with his empty tucker-bags;
And I fancy that of evenings, when the track is growing dim,
What he 'might have been and wasn't' comes along and troubles him.

Middleton's Rouseabout

Tall and freckled and sandy,
Face of a country lout;
This was the picture of Andy,
Middleton's Rouseabout.

Type of a coming nation,

In the land of cattle and sheep,
Worked on Middleton's station,
'Pound a week and his keep.'

On Middleton's wide dominions
Plied the stockwhip and shears;
Hadn't any opinions,
Hadn't any 'idears'.

Swiftly the years went over,
Liquor and drought prevailed;
Middleton went as a drover,
After his station had failed.

Type of a careless nation,
Men who are soon played out,
Middleton was: — and his station
Was bought by the Rouseabout.

Flourishing beard and sandy,
Tall and robust and stout;
This is the picture of Andy,
Middleton's Rouseabout.

Now on his own dominions
Works with his overseers;
Hasn't any opinions,
Hasn't any 'idears'.

The Ballad of the Drover

Across the stony ridges,
Across the rolling plain,
Young Harry Dale, the drover,
Comes riding home again.
And well his stock-horse bears him,
And light of heart is he,
And stoutly his old pack-horse
Is trotting by his knee.

Up Queensland way with cattle
He travelled regions vast;
And many months have vanished
Since home-folk saw him last.
He hums a song of someone
He hopes to marry soon;

And hobble-chains and camp-ware
Keep jingling to the tune.

Beyond the hazy dado
Against the lower skies
And yon blue line of ranges
The homestead station lies.
And thitherward the drover
Jogs through the lazy noon,
While hobble-chains and camp-ware
Are jingling to a tune.

An hour has filled the heavens
With storm-clouds inky black;
At times the lightning trickles
Around the drover's track;
But Harry pushes onward,
His horses' strength he tries,
In hope to reach the river
Before the flood shall rise.

The thunder from above him
Goes rolling o'er the plain;
And down on thirsty pastures
In torrents falls the rain.
And every creek and gully
Sends forth its little flood,
Till the river runs a banker,
All stained with yellow mud.

Now Harry speaks to Rover,
The best dog on the plains,
And to his hardy horses,
And strokes their shaggy manes;
'We've breasted bigger rivers
When floods were at their height
Nor shall this gutter stop us
From getting home to-night!'

The thunder growls a warning,
The ghastly lightnings gleam,
As the drover turns his horses
To swim the fatal stream.
But, oh! the flood runs stronger
Than e'er it ran before;
The saddle-horse is failing,
And only half-way o'er!

When flashes next the lightning,
The flood's grey breast is blank,
And a cattle dog and pack-horse
Are struggling up the bank.
But in the lonely homestead
The girl will wait in vain —
He'll never pass the stations
In charge of stock again.

The faithful dog a moment
Sits panting on the bank,
And then swims through the current
To where his master sank.
And round and round in circles
He fights with failing strength,
Till, borne down by the waters,
The old dog sinks at length.

Across the flooded lowlands
And slopes of sodden loam
The pack-horse struggles onward,
To take dumb tidings home.
And mud-stained, wet, and weary,
Through ranges dark goes he;
While hobble-chains and tinware
Are sounding eerily.

The floods are in the ocean,
The stream is clear again,
And now a verdant carpet
Is stretched across the plain.
But someone's eyes are saddened,
And someone's heart still bleeds
In sorrow for the drover
Who sleeps among the reeds.

Taking His Chance

They stood by the door of the Inn on the Rise;
May Carney looked up in the bushranger's eyes:
'Oh! why did you come? — it was mad of you, Jack;
You know that the troopers are out on your track.'
A laugh and a shake of his obstinate head —
'I wanted a dance, and I'll chance it,' he said.

Some twenty-odd bushmen had come to the 'ball',

But Jack from his youth had been known to them all,
And bushmen are soft where a woman is fair,
So the love of May Carney protected him there;
And all the short evening — it seems like romance —
She danced with a bushranger taking his chance.

'Twas midnight — the dancers stood suddenly still,
For hoofs had been heard on the side of the hill!
Ben Duggan, the drover, along the hillside
Came riding as only a bushman can ride.
He sprang from his horse, to the shanty he sped —
'The troopers are down in the gully!' he said.

Quite close to the homestead the troopers were seen.
'Clear out and ride hard for the ranges, Jack Dean!
Be quick!' said May Carney — her hand on her heart —
'We'll bluff them awhile, and 'twill give you a start.'
He lingered a moment — to kiss her, of course —
Then ran to the trees where he'd hobbled his horse.

She ran to the gate, and the troopers were there —
The jingle of hobbles came faint on the air —
Then loudly she screamed: it was only to drown
The treacherous clatter of slip-rails let down.
But troopers are sharp, and she saw at a glance
That someone was taking a desperate chance.

They chased, and they shouted, 'Surrender, Jack Dean!'
They called him three times in the name of the Queen.
Then came from the darkness the clicking of locks;
The crack of the rifles was heard in the rocks!
A shriek and a shout, and a rush of pale men —
And there lay the bushranger, chancing it then.

The sergeant dismounted and knelt on the sod —
'Your bushranging's over — make peace, Jack, with God!'
The bushranger laughed — not a word he replied,
But turned to the girl who knelt down by his side.
He gazed in her eyes as she lifted his head:
'Just kiss me — my girl — and — I'll — chance it,' he said.

When the 'Army' Prays for Watty

When the kindly hours of darkness, save for light of moon and star,
Hide the picture on the signboard over Doughty's Horse Bazaar;
When the last rose-tint is fading on the distant mulga scrub,

Then the Army prays for Watty at the entrance of his pub.

Now, I often sit at Watty's when the night is very near,
With a head that's full of jingles and the fumes of bottled beer,
For I always have a fancy that, if I am over there
When the Army prays for Watty, I'm included in the prayer.

Watty lounges in his arm-chair, in its old accustomed place,
With a fatherly expression on his round and passive face;
And his arms are clasped before him in a calm, contented way,
And he nods his head and dozes when he hears the Army pray.

And I wonder does he ponder on the distant years and dim,
Or his chances over yonder, when the Army prays for him?
Has he not a fear connected with the warm place down below,
Where, according to good Christians, all the publicans should go?

But his features give no token of a feeling in his breast,
Save of peace that is unbroken and a conscience well at rest;
And we guzzle as we guzzled long before the Army came,
And the loafers wait for 'shouters' and — they get there just the same.

It would take a lot of praying — lots of thumping on the drum —
To prepare our sinful, straying, erring souls for Kingdom Come;
But I love my fellow-sinners, and I hope, upon the whole,
That the Army gets a hearing when it prays for Watty's soul.

The Wreck of the 'Derry Castle'

Day of ending for beginnings!
Ocean hath another innings,
Ocean hath another score;
And the surges sing his winnings,
And the surges shout his winnings,
And the surges shriek his winnings,
All along the sullen shore.

Sing another dirge in wailing,
For another vessel sailing
With the shadow-ships at sea;
Shadow-ships for ever sinking —
Shadow-ships whose pumps are clinking,
And whose thirsty holds are drinking
Pledges to Eternity.

Pray for souls of ghastly, sodden

Corpses, floating round untrodden
Cliffs, where nought but sea-drift strays;
Souls of dead men, in whose faces
Of humanity no trace is —
Not a mark to show their races —
Floating round for days and days.

Ocean's salty tongues are licking
Round the faces of the drowned,
And a cruel blade seems sticking
Through my heart and turning round.

Heaven! shall HIS ghastly, sodden
Corpse float round for days and days?
Shall it dash 'neath cliffs untrodden,
Rocks where nought but sea-drift strays?

God in heaven! hide the floating,
Falling, rising, face from me;
God in heaven! stay the gloating,
Mocking singing of the sea!

Ben Duggan

Jack Denver died on Talbragar when Christmas Eve began,
And there was sorrow round the place, for Denver was a man;
Jack Denver's wife bowed down her head — her daughter's grief was wild,
And big Ben Duggan by the bed stood sobbing like a child.
But big Ben Duggan saddled up, and galloped fast and far,
To raise the longest funeral ever seen on Talbragar.

By station home
And shearing shed
Ben Duggan cried, 'Jack Denver's dead!
Roll up at Talbragar!'

He borrowed horses here and there, and rode all Christmas Eve,
And scarcely paused a moment's time the mournful news to leave;
He rode by lonely huts and farms, and when the day was done
He turned his panting horse's head and rode to Ross's Run.
No bushman in a single day had ridden half so far
Since Johnson brought the doctor to his wife at Talbragar.

By diggers' camps
Ben Duggan sped —
At each he cried, 'Jack Denver's dead!

Roll up at Talbragar!'

That night he passed the humpies of the splitters on the ridge,
And roused the bullock-drivers camped at Belinfante's Bridge;
And as he climbed the ridge again the moon shone on the rise;
The soft white moonbeams glistened in the tears that filled his eyes;
He dashed the rebel drops away — for blinding things they are —
But 'twas his best and truest friend who died on Talbragar.

At Blackman's Run
Before the dawn,
Ben Duggan cried, 'Poor Denver's gone!
Roll up at Talbragar!'

At all the shanties round the place they'd heard his horse's tramp,
He took the track to Wilson's Luck, and told the diggers' camp;
But in the gorge by Deadman's Gap the mountain shades were black,
And there a newly-fallen tree was lying on the track —
He saw too late, and then he heard the swift hoof's sudden jar,
And big Ben Duggan ne'er again rode home to Talbragar.

'The wretch is drunk,
And Denver's dead —
A burning shame!' the people said
Next day at Talbragar.

For thirty miles round Talbragar the boys rolled up in strength,
And Denver had a funeral a good long mile in length;
Round Denver's grave that Christmas day rough bushmen's eyes were dim —
The western bushmen knew the way to bury dead like him;
But some returning homeward found, by light of moon and star,
Ben Duggan dying in the rocks, five miles from Talbragar.

They knelt around,
He raised his head
And faintly gasped, 'Jack Denver's dead,
Roll up at Talbragar!'

But one short hour before he died he woke to understand,
They told him, when he asked them, that the funeral was 'grand';
And then there came into his eyes a strange victorious light,
He smiled on them in triumph, and his great soul took its flight.
And still the careless bushmen tell by tent and shanty bar
How Duggan raised a funeral years back on Talbragar.

And far and wide
When Duggan died,
The bushmen of the western side

Rode in to Talbragar.

We boast no more of our bloodless flag, that rose from a nation's slime;
Better a shred of a deep-dyed rag from the storms of the olden time.
From grander clouds in our 'peaceful skies' than ever were there before
I tell you the Star of the South shall rise — in the lurid clouds of war.
It ever must be while blood is warm and the sons of men increase;
For ever the nations rose in storm, to rot in a deadly peace.
There comes a point that we will not yield, no matter if right or wrong,
And man will fight on the battle-field
while passion and pride are strong —
So long as he will not kiss the rod, and his stubborn spirit sours,
And the scorn of Nature and curse of God are heavy on peace like ours.

There are boys out there by the western creeks, who hurry away from school
To climb the sides of the breezy peaks or dive in the shaded pool,
Who'll stick to their guns when the mountains quake to the tread of a mighty war,
And fight for Right or a Grand Mistake as men never fought before;
When the peaks are scarred and the sea-walls crack till the furthest hills vibrate,
And the world for a while goes rolling back in a storm of love and hate.

There are boys to-day in the city slum and the home of wealth and pride
Who'll have one home when the storm is come, and fight for it side by side,
Who'll hold the cliffs 'gainst the armoured hells that batter a coastal town,
Or grimly die in a hail of shells when the walls come crashing down.
And many a pink-white baby girl, the queen of her home to-day,
Shall see the wings of the tempest whirl the mist of our dawn away —
Shall live to shudder and stop her ears to the thud of the distant gun,
And know the sorrow that has no tears when a battle is lost and won, —
As a mother or wife in the years to come, will kneel, wild-eyed and white,
And pray to God in her darkened home for the 'men in the fort to-night'.

But, oh! if the cavalry charge again as they did when the world was wide,
'Twill be grand in the ranks of a thousand men in that glorious race to ride
And strike for all that is true and strong, for all that is grand and brave,
And all that ever shall be, so long as man has a soul to save.
He must lift the saddle, and close his 'wings', and shut his angels out,
And steel his heart for the end of things, who'd ride with a stockman scout,
When the race they ride on the battle track, and the waning distance hums,
And the shelled sky shrieks or the rifles crack like stockwhip amongst the gums —
And the 'straight' is reached and the field is 'gapped' and the hoof-torn sward grows red
With the blood of those who are handicapped with iron and steel and lead;
And the gaps are filled, though unseen by eyes, with the spirit and with the shades

Of the world-wide rebel dead who'll rise and rush with the Bush Brigades.

All creeds and trades will have soldiers there — give every class its due —
And there'll be many a clerk to spare for the pride of the jackeroo.
They'll fight for honour and fight for love, and a few will fight for gold,
For the devil below and for God above, as our fathers fought of old;
And some half-blind with exultant tears, and some stiff-lipped, stern-eyed,
For the pride of a thousand after-years and the old eternal pride;
The soul of the world they will feel and see in the chase and the grim retreat —
They'll know the glory of victory — and the grandeur of defeat.

The South will wake to a mighty change ere a hundred years are done
With arsenals west of the mountain range and every spur its gun.
And many a rickety son of a gun, on the tides of the future tossed,
Will tell how battles were really won that History says were lost,
Will trace the field with his pipe, and shirk the facts that are hard to explain,
As grey old mates of the diggings work the old ground over again —
How 'this was our centre, and this a redoubt, and that was a scrub in the rear,
And this was the point where the guards held out, and the enemy's lines were here.'

They'll tell the tales of the nights before and the tales of the ship and fort
Till the sons of Australia take to war as their fathers took to sport,
Their breath come deep and their eyes grow bright at the tales of our chivalry,
And every boy will want to fight, no matter what cause it be —
When the children run to the doors and cry:
'Oh, mother, the troops are come!'
And every heart in the town leaps high at the first loud thud of the drum.
They'll know, apart from its mystic charm, what music is at last,
When, proud as a boy with a broken arm, the regiment marches past.
And the veriest wreck in the drink-fiend's clutch, no matter how low or mean,
Will feel, when he hears the march, a touch of the man that he might have been.
And fools, when the fiends of war are out and the city skies aflame,
Will have something better to talk about than an absent woman's shame,
Will have something nobler to do by far than jest at a friend's expense,
Or blacken a name in a public bar or over a backyard fence.
And this you learn from the libelled past, though its methods were somewhat rude —
A nation's born where the shells fall fast, or its lease of life renewed.
We in part atone for the ghoulish strife, and the crimes of the peace we boast,
And the better part of a people's life in the storm comes uppermost.

The self-same spirit that drives the man to the depths of drink and crime
Will do the deeds in the heroes' van that live till the end of time.
The living death in the lonely bush, the greed of the selfish town,
And even the creed of the outlawed push is chivalry — upside down.
'Twill be while ever our blood is hot, while ever the world goes wrong,
The nations rise in a war, to rot in a peace that lasts too long.
And southern nation and southern state, aroused from their dream of ease,
Must sign in the Book of Eternal Fate their stormy histories.

The Great Grey Plain

Out West, where the stars are brightest,
Where the scorching north wind blows,
And the bones of the dead gleam whitest,
And the sun on a desert glows —
Yet within the selfish kingdom
Where man starves man for gain,
Where white men tramp for existence —
Wide lies the Great Grey Plain.

No break in its awful horizon,
No blur in the dazzling haze,
Save where by the bordering timber
The fierce, white heat-waves blaze,
And out where the tank-heap rises
Or looms when the sunlights wane,
Till it seems like a distant mountain
Low down on the Great Grey Plain.

No sign of a stream or fountain,
No spring on its dry, hot breast,
No shade from the blazing noontide
Where a weary man might rest.
Whole years go by when the glowing
Sky never clouds for rain —
Only the shrubs of the desert
Grow on the Great Grey Plain.

From the camp, while the rich man's dreaming,
Come the 'traveller' and his mate,
In the ghastly dawnlight seeming
Like a swagman's ghost out late;
And the horseman blurs in the distance,
While still the stars remain,
A low, faint dust-cloud haunting
His track on the Great Grey Plain.

And all day long from before them
The mirage smokes away —
That daylight ghost of an ocean
Creeps close behind all day
With an evil, snake-like motion,
As the waves of a madman's brain:
'Tis a phantom NOT like water

Out there on the Great Grey Plain.

There's a run on the Western limit
Where a man lives like a beast,
And a shanty in the mulga
That stretches to the East;
And the hopeless men who carry
Their swags and tramp in pain —
The footmen must not tarry
Out there on the Great Grey Plain.

Out West, where the stars are brightest,
Where the scorching north wind blows,
And the bones of the dead seem whitest,
And the sun on a desert glows —
Out back in the hungry distance
That brave hearts dare in vain —
Where beggars tramp for existence —
There lies the Great Grey Plain.

'Tis a desert not more barren
Than the Great Grey Plain of years,
Where a fierce fire burns the hearts of men —
Dries up the fount of tears:
Where the victims of a greed insane
Are crushed in a hell-born strife —
Where the souls of a race are murdered
On the Great Grey Plain of Life!

The Song of Old Joe Swallow

When I was up the country in the rough and early days,
I used to work along ov Jimmy Nowlett's bullick-drays;
Then the reelroad wasn't heered on, an' the bush was wild an' strange,
An' we useter draw the timber from the saw-pits in the range —
Load provisions for the stations, an' we'd travel far and slow
Through the plains an' 'cross the ranges in the days of long ago.

Then it's yoke up the bullicks and tramp beside 'em slow,
An' saddle up yer horses an' a-ridin' we will go,
To the bullick-drivin', cattle-drovin',
Nigger, digger, roarin', rovin'
Days o' long ago.

Once me and Jimmy Nowlett loaded timber for the town,
But we hadn't gone a dozen mile before the rain come down,

An' me an' Jimmy Nowlett an' the bullicks an' the dray
Was cut off on some risin' ground while floods around us lay;
An' we soon run short of tucker an' terbacca, which was bad,
An' pertaters dipped in honey was the only tuck we had.

An' half our bullicks perished when the drought was on the land,
An' the burnin' heat that dazzles as it dances on the sand;
When the sun-baked clay an' gravel paves for miles the burnin' creeks,
An' at ev'ry step yer travel there a rottin' carcase reeks —
But we pulled ourselves together, for we never used ter know
What a feather bed was good for in those days o' long ago.

But in spite ov barren ridges an' in spite ov mud an' heat,
An' dust that browned the bushes when it rose from bullicks' feet,
An' in spite ov cold and chilblains when the bush was white with frost,
An' in spite of muddy water where the burnin' plain was crossed,
An' in spite of modern progress, and in spite of all their blow,
'Twas a better land to live in, in the days o' long ago.

When the frosty moon was shinin' o'er the ranges like a lamp,
An' a lot of bullick-drivers was a-campin' on the camp,
When the fire was blazin' cheery an' the pipes was drawin' well,
Then our songs we useter chorus an' our yarns we useter tell;
An' we'd talk ov lands we come from, and ov chaps we useter know,
For there always was behind us OTHER days o' long ago.

Ah, them early days was ended when the reelroad crossed the plain,
But in dreams I often tramp beside the bullick-team again:
Still we pauses at the shanty just to have a drop er cheer,
Still I feels a kind ov pleasure when the campin'-ground is near;
Still I smells the old tarpaulin me an' Jimmy useter throw
O'er the timber-truck for shelter in the days ov long ago.

I have been a-driftin' back'ards with the changes ov the land,
An' if I spoke ter bullicks now they wouldn't understand,
But when Mary wakes me sudden in the night I'll often say:
'Come here, Spot, an' stan' up, Bally, blank an' blank an' come-eer-way.'
An' she says that, when I'm sleepin', oft my elerquince 'ill flow
In the bullick-drivin' language ov the days o' long ago.

Well, the pub will soon be closin', so I'll give the thing a rest;
But if you should drop on Nowlett in the far an' distant west —
An' if Jimmy uses doubleyou instead of ar an' vee,
An' if he drops his aitches, then you're sure to know it's he.
An' yer won't forgit to arsk him if he still remembers Joe
As knowed him up the country in the days o' long ago.

Then it's yoke up the bullicks and tramp beside 'em slow,

An' saddle up yer horses an' a-ridin' we will go,
To the bullick-drivin', cattle-drovin',
Nigger, digger, roarin', rovin'
Days o' long ago.

Corny Bill

His old clay pipe stuck in his mouth,
His hat pushed from his brow,
His dress best fitted for the South —
I think I see him now;
And when the city streets are still,
And sleep upon me comes,
I often dream that me an' Bill
Are humpin' of our drums.

I mind the time when first I came
A stranger to the land;
And I was stumped, an' sick, an' lame
When Bill took me in hand.
Old Bill was what a chap would call
A friend in poverty,
And he was very kind to all,
And very good to me.

We'd camp beneath the lonely trees
And sit beside the blaze,
A-nursin' of our wearied knees,
A-smokin' of our clays.
Or when we'd journeyed damp an' far,
An' clouds were in the skies,
We'd camp in some old shanty bar,
And sit a-tellin' lies.

Though time had writ upon his brow
And rubbed away his curls,
He always was — an' may be now —
A favourite with the girls;
I've heard bush-wimmin scream an' squall —
I've see'd 'em laugh until
They could not do their work at all,
Because of Corny Bill.

He was the jolliest old pup
As ever you did see,
And often at some bush kick-up

They'd make old Bill M.C.
He'd make them dance and sing all night,
He'd make the music hum,
But he'd be gone at mornin' light
A-humpin' of his drum.

Though joys of which the poet rhymes
Was not for Bill an' me,
I think we had some good old times
Out on the wallaby.
I took a wife and left off rum,
An' camped beneath a roof;
But Bill preferred to hump his drum
A-paddin' of the hoof.

The lazy, idle loafers what
In toney houses camp
Would call old Bill a drunken sot,
A loafer, or a tramp;
But if the dead should ever dance —
As poets say they will —
I think I'd rather take my chance
Along of Corny Bill.

His long life's-day is nearly o'er,
Its shades begin to fall;
He soon must mount his bluey for
The last long tramp of all;
I trust that when, in bush an' town,
He's lived and learnt his fill,
They'll let the golden slip-rails down
For poor old Corny Bill.

Cherry-Tree Inn

The rafters are open to sun, moon, and star,
Thistles and nettles grow high in the bar —
The chimneys are crumbling, the log fires are dead,
And green mosses spring from the hearthstone instead.
The voices are silent, the bustle and din,
For the railroad hath ruined the Cherry-tree Inn.

Save the glimmer of stars, or the moon's pallid streams,
And the sounds of the 'possums that camp on the beams,
The bar-room is dark and the stable is still,
For the coach comes no more over Cherry-tree Hill.

No riders push on through the darkness to win
The rest and the comfort of Cherry-tree Inn.

I drift from my theme, for my memory strays
To the carrying, digging, and bushranging days —
Far back to the seasons that I love the best,
When a stream of wild diggers rushed into the west,
But the 'rushes' grew feeble, and sluggish, and thin,
Till scarcely a swagman passed Cherry-tree Inn.

Do you think, my old mate (if it's thinking you be),
Of the days when you tramped to the goldfields with me?
Do you think of the day of our thirty-mile tramp,
When never a fire could we light on the camp,
And, weary and footsore and drenched to the skin,
We tramped through the darkness to Cherry-tree Inn?

Then I had a sweetheart and you had a wife,
And Johnny was more to his mother than life;
But we solemnly swore, ere that evening was done,
That we'd never return till our fortunes were won.
Next morning to harvests of folly and sin
We tramped o'er the ranges from Cherry-tree Inn.

The years have gone over with many a change,
And there comes an old swagman from over the range,
And faint 'neath the weight of his rain-sodden load,
He suddenly thinks of the inn by the road.
He tramps through the darkness the shelter to win,
And reaches the ruins of Cherry-tree Inn.

Up the Country

I am back from up the country — very sorry that I went —
Seeking for the Southern poets' land whereon to pitch my tent;
I have lost a lot of idols, which were broken on the track,
Burnt a lot of fancy verses, and I'm glad that I am back.
Further out may be the pleasant scenes of which our poets boast,
But I think the country's rather more inviting round the coast.
Anyway, I'll stay at present at a boarding-house in town,
Drinking beer and lemon-squashes, taking baths and cooling down.

'Sunny plains'! Great Scott! — those burning wastes of barren soil and sand
With their everlasting fences stretching out across the land!
Desolation where the crow is! Desert where the eagle flies,
Paddocks where the luny bullock starts and stares with reddened eyes;

Where, in clouds of dust enveloped, roasted bullock-drivers creep
Slowly past the sun-dried shepherd dragged behind his crawling sheep.
Stunted peak of granite gleaming, glaring like a molten mass
Turned from some infernal furnace on a plain devoid of grass.

Miles and miles of thirsty gutters — strings of muddy water-holes
In the place of 'shining rivers' — 'walled by cliffs and forest boles.'
Barren ridges, gullies, ridges! where the ever-madd'ning flies —
Fiercer than the plagues of Egypt — swarm about your blighted eyes!
Bush! where there is no horizon! where the buried bushman sees
Nothing — Nothing! but the sameness of the ragged, stunted trees!
Lonely hut where drought's eternal, suffocating atmosphere
Where the God-forgotten hatter dreams of city life and beer.

Treacherous tracks that trap the stranger, endless roads that gleam and glare,
Dark and evil-looking gullies, hiding secrets here and there!
Dull dumb flats and stony rises, where the toiling bullocks bake,
And the sinister 'gohanna', and the lizard, and the snake.
Land of day and night — no morning freshness, and no afternoon,
When the great white sun in rising bringeth summer heat in June.
Dismal country for the exile, when the shades begin to fall
From the sad heart-breaking sunset, to the new-chum worst of all.

Dreary land in rainy weather, with the endless clouds that drift
O'er the bushman like a blanket that the Lord will never lift —
Dismal land when it is raining — growl of floods, and, oh! the woosh
Of the rain and wind together on the dark bed of the bush —
Ghastly fires in lonely humpies where the granite rocks are piled
In the rain-swept wildernesses that are wildest of the wild.

Land where gaunt and haggard women live alone and work like men,
Till their husbands, gone a-droving, will return to them again:
Homes of men! if home had ever such a God-forgotten place,
Where the wild selector's children fly before a stranger's face.
Home of tragedy applauded by the dingoes' dismal yell,
Heaven of the shanty-keeper — fitting fiend for such a hell —
And the wallaroos and wombats, and, of course, the curlew's call —
And the lone sundowner tramping ever onward through it all!

I am back from up the country, up the country where I went
Seeking for the Southern poets' land whereon to pitch my tent;
I have shattered many idols out along the dusty track,
Burnt a lot of fancy verses — and I'm glad that I am back.
I believe the Southern poets' dream will not be realised
Till the plains are irrigated and the land is humanised.
I intend to stay at present, as I said before, in town
Drinking beer and lemon-squashes, taking baths and cooling down.

Knocked Up

I'm lyin' on the barren ground that's baked and cracked with drought,
And dunno if my legs or back or heart is most wore out;
I've got no spirits left to rise and smooth me achin' brow —
I'm too knocked up to light a fire and bile the billy now.

Oh it's trampin', trampin', tra-a-mpin', in flies an' dust an' heat,
Or it's trampin' trampin' tra-a-a-mpin' through mud and slush 'n sleet;
It's tramp an' tramp for tucker — one everlastin' strife,
An' wearin' out yer boots an' heart in the wastin' of yer life.

They whine o' lost an' wasted lives in idleness and crime —
I've wasted mine for twenty years, and grafted all the time
And never drunk the stuff I earned, nor gambled when I shore —
But somehow when yer on the track yer life seems wasted more.

A long dry stretch of thirty miles I've tramped this broilin' day,
All for the off-chance of a job a hundred miles away;
There's twenty hungry beggars wild for any job this year,
An' fifty might be at the shed while I am lyin' here.

The sinews in my legs seem drawn, red-hot — 'n that's the truth;
I seem to weigh a ton, and ache like one tremendous tooth;
I'm stung between my shoulder-blades — my blessed back seems broke;
I'm too knocked out to eat a bite — I'm too knocked up to smoke.

The blessed rain is comin' too — there's oceans in the sky,
An' I suppose I must get up and rig the blessed fly;
The heat is bad, the water's bad, the flies a crimson curse,
The grub is bad, mosquitoes damned — but rheumatism's worse.

I wonder why poor blokes like me will stick so fast ter breath,
Though Shakespeare says it is the fear of somethin' after death;
But though Eternity be cursed with God's almighty curse —
What ever that same somethin' is I swear it can't be worse.

For it's trampin', trampin', tra-a-mpin' thro' hell across the plain,
And it's trampin' trampin' tra-a-mpin' thro' slush 'n mud 'n rain —
A livin' worse than any dog — without a home 'n wife,
A-wearin' out yer heart 'n soul in the wastin' of yer life.

The Blue Mountains

Above the ashes straight and tall,
Through ferns with moisture dripping,
I climb beneath the sandstone wall,
My feet on mosses slipping.

Like ramparts round the valley's edge
The tinted cliffs are standing,
With many a broken wall and ledge,
And many a rocky landing.

And round about their rugged feet
Deep ferny dells are hidden
In shadowed depths, whence dust and heat
Are banished and forbidden.

The stream that, crooning to itself,
Comes down a tireless rover,
Flows calmly to the rocky shelf,
And there leaps bravely over.

Now pouring down, now lost in spray
When mountain breezes sally,
The water strikes the rock midway,
And leaps into the valley.

Now in the west the colours change,
The blue with crimson blending;
Behind the far Dividing Range,
The sun is fast descending.

And mellowed day comes o'er the place,
And softens ragged edges;
The rising moon's great placid face
Looks gravely o'er the ledges.

The City Bushman

It was pleasant up the country, City Bushman, where you went,
For you sought the greener patches and you travelled like a gent;
And you curse the trams and buses and the turmoil and the push,
Though you know the squalid city needn't keep you from the bush;
But we lately heard you singing of the 'plains where shade is not',
And you mentioned it was dusty — 'all was dry and all was hot'.

True, the bush 'hath moods and changes' — and the bushman hath 'em, too,
For he's not a poet's dummy — he's a man, the same as you;

But his back is growing rounder — slaving for the absentee —
And his toiling wife is thinner than a country wife should be.
For we noticed that the faces of the folks we chanced to meet
Should have made a greater contrast to the faces in the street;
And, in short, we think the bushman's being driven to the wall,
And it's doubtful if his spirit will be 'loyal thro' it all'.

Though the bush has been romantic and it's nice to sing about,
There's a lot of patriotism that the land could do without —
Sort of BRITISH WORKMAN nonsense that shall perish in the scorn
Of the drover who is driven and the shearer who is shorn,
Of the struggling western farmers who have little time for rest,
And are ruined on selections in the sheep-infested West;
Droving songs are very pretty, but they merit little thanks
From the people of a country in possession of the Banks.

And the 'rise and fall of seasons' suits the rise and fall of rhyme,
But we know that western seasons do not run on schedule time;
For the drought will go on drying while there's anything to dry,
Then it rains until you'd fancy it would bleach the sunny sky —
Then it pelters out of reason, for the downpour day and night
Nearly sweeps the population to the Great Australian Bight.
It is up in Northern Queensland that the seasons do their best,
But it's doubtful if you ever saw a season in the West;
There are years without an autumn or a winter or a spring,
There are broiling Junes, and summers when it rains like anything.

In the bush my ears were opened to the singing of the bird,
But the 'carol of the magpie' was a thing I never heard.
Once the beggar roused my slumbers in a shanty, it is true,
But I only heard him asking, 'Who the blanky blank are you?'
And the bell-bird in the ranges — but his 'silver chime' is harsh
When it's heard beside the solo of the curlew in the marsh.

Yes, I heard the shearers singing 'William Riley', out of tune,
Saw 'em fighting round a shanty on a Sunday afternoon,
But the bushman isn't always 'trapping brumbies in the night',
Nor is he for ever riding when 'the morn is fresh and bright',
And he isn't always singing in the humpies on the run —
And the camp-fire's 'cheery blazes' are a trifle overdone;
We have grumbled with the bushmen round the fire on rainy days,
When the smoke would blind a bullock and there wasn't any blaze,
Save the blazes of our language, for we cursed the fire in turn
Till the atmosphere was heated and the wood began to burn.
Then we had to wring our blueys which were rotting in the swags,
And we saw the sugar leaking through the bottoms of the bags,
And we couldn't raise a chorus, for the toothache and the cramp,
While we spent the hours of darkness draining puddles round the camp.

Would you like to change with Clancy — go a-droving? tell us true,
For we rather think that Clancy would be glad to change with you,
And be something in the city; but 'twould give your muse a shock
To be losing time and money through the foot-rot in the flock,
And you wouldn't mind the beauties underneath the starry dome
If you had a wife and children and a lot of bills at home.

Did you ever guard the cattle when the night was inky-black,
And it rained, and icy water trickled gently down your back
Till your saddle-weary backbone fell a-aching to the roots
And you almost felt the croaking of the bull-frog in your boots —
Sit and shiver in the saddle, curse the restless stock and cough
Till a squatter's irate dummy cantered up to warn you off?
Did you fight the drought and pleuro when the 'seasons' were asleep,
Felling sheoaks all the morning for a flock of starving sheep,
Drinking mud instead of water — climbing trees and lopping boughs
For the broken-hearted bullocks and the dry and dusty cows?

Do you think the bush was better in the 'good old droving days',
When the squatter ruled supremely as the king of western ways,
When you got a slip of paper for the little you could earn,
But were forced to take provisions from the station in return —
When you couldn't keep a chicken at your humpy on the run,
For the squatter wouldn't let you — and your work was never done;
When you had to leave the missus in a lonely hut forlorn
While you 'rose up Willy Riley' — in the days ere you were born?

Ah! we read about the drovers and the shearers and the like
Till we wonder why such happy and romantic fellows strike.
Don't you fancy that the poets ought to give the bush a rest
Ere they raise a just rebellion in the over-written West?
Where the simple-minded bushman gets a meal and bed and rum
Just by riding round reporting phantom flocks that never come;
Where the scalper — never troubled by the 'war-whoop of the push' —
Has a quiet little billet — breeding rabbits in the bush;
Where the idle shanty-keeper never fails to make a draw,
And the dummy gets his tucker through provisions in the law;
Where the labour-agitator — when the shearers rise in might —
Makes his money sacrificing all his substance for The Right;
Where the squatter makes his fortune, and 'the seasons rise and fall',
And the poor and honest bushman has to suffer for it all;
Where the drovers and the shearers and the bushmen and the rest
Never reach the Eldorado of the poets of the West.

And you think the bush is purer and that life is better there,
But it doesn't seem to pay you like the 'squalid street and square'.
Pray inform us, City Bushman, where you read, in prose or verse,

Of the awful 'city urchin who would greet you with a curse'.
There are golden hearts in gutters, though their owners lack the fat,
And we'll back a teamster's offspring to outswear a city brat.
Do you think we're never jolly where the trams and buses rage?
Did you hear the gods in chorus when 'Ri-tooral' held the stage?
Did you catch a ring of sorrow in the city urchin's voice
When he yelled for Billy Elton, when he thumped the floor for Royce?
Do the bushmen, down on pleasure, miss the everlasting stars
When they drink and flirt and so on in the glow of private bars?

You've a down on 'trams and buses', or the 'roar' of 'em, you said,
And the 'filthy, dirty attic', where you never toiled for bread.
(And about that self-same attic — Lord! wherever have you been?
For the struggling needlewoman mostly keeps her attic clean.)
But you'll find it very jolly with the cuff-and-collar push,
And the city seems to suit you, while you rave about the bush.

You'll admit that Up-the Country, more especially in drought,
Isn't quite the Eldorado that the poets rave about,
Yet at times we long to gallop where the reckless bushman rides
In the wake of startled brumbies that are flying for their hides;
Long to feel the saddle tremble once again between our knees
And to hear the stockwhips rattle just like rifles in the trees!
Long to feel the bridle-leather tugging strongly in the hand
And to feel once more a little like a native of the land.
And the ring of bitter feeling in the jingling of our rhymes
Isn't suited to the country nor the spirit of the times.
Let us go together droving, and returning, if we live,
Try to understand each other while we reckon up the div.

Eurunderee

There are scenes in the distance where beauty is not,
On the desolate flats where gaunt appletrees rot.
Where the brooding old ridge rises up to the breeze
From his dark lonely gullies of stringy-bark trees,
There are voice-haunted gaps, ever sullen and strange,
But Eurunderee lies like a gem in the range.

Still I see in my fancy the dark-green and blue
Of the box-covered hills where the five-corners grew;
And the rugged old sheoaks that sighed in the bend
O'er the lily-decked pools where the dark ridges end,
And the scrub-covered spurs running down from the Peak
To the deep grassy banks of Eurunderee Creek.

On the knolls where the vineyards and fruit-gardens are
There's a beauty that even the drought cannot mar;
For I noticed it oft, in the days that are lost,
As I trod on the siding where lingered the frost,
When the shadows of night from the gullies were gone
And the hills in the background were flushed by the dawn.

I was there in late years, but there's many a change
Where the Cudgegong River flows down through the range,
For the curse of the town with the railroad had come,
And the goldfields were dead. And the girl and the chum
And the old home were gone, yet the oaks seemed to speak
Of the hazy old days on Eurunderee Creek.

And I stood by that creek, ere the sunset grew cold,
When the leaves of the sheoaks are traced on the gold,
And I thought of old things, and I thought of old folks,
Till I sighed in my heart to the sigh of the oaks;
For the years waste away like the waters that leak
Through the pebbles and sand of Eurunderee Creek.

Mount Bukaroo

Only one old post is standing —
Solid yet, but only one —
Where the milking, and the branding,
And the slaughtering were done.
Later years have brought dejection,
Care, and sorrow; but we knew
Happy days on that selection
Underneath old Bukaroo.

Then the light of day commencing
Found us at the gully's head,
Splitting timber for the fencing,
Stripping bark to roof the shed.
Hands and hearts the labour strengthened;
Weariness we never knew,
Even when the shadows lengthened
Round the base of Bukaroo.

There for days below the paddock
How the wilderness would yield
To the spade, and pick, and mattock,
While we toiled to win the field.
Bronzed hands we used to sully

Till they were of darkest hue,
'Burning off' down in the gully
At the back of Bukaroo.

When we came the baby brother
Left in haste his broken toys,
Shouted to the busy mother:
'Here is dadda and the boys!'
Strange it seems that she was able
For the work that she would do;
How she'd bustle round the table
In the hut 'neath Bukaroo!

When the cows were safely yarded,
And the calves were in the pen,
All the cares of day discarded,
Closed we round the hut-fire then.
Rang the roof with boyish laughter
While the flames o'er-topped the flue;
Happy days remembered after —
Far away from Bukaroo.

But the years were full of changes,
And a sorrow found us there;
For our home amid the ranges
Was not safe from searching Care.
On he came, a silent creeper;
And another mountain threw
O'er our lives a shadow deeper
Than the shade of Bukaroo.

All the farm is disappearing;
For the home has vanished now,
Mountain scrub has choked the clearing,
Hid the furrows of the plough.
Nearer still the scrub is creeping
Where the little garden grew;
And the old folks now are sleeping
At the foot of Bukaroo.

The Fire at Ross's Farm

The squatter saw his pastures wide
Decrease, as one by one
The farmers moving to the west
Selected on his run;

Selectors took the water up
And all the black soil round;
The best grass-land the squatter had
Was spoilt by Ross's Ground.

Now many schemes to shift old Ross
Had racked the squatter's brains,
But Sandy had the stubborn blood
Of Scotland in his veins;
He held the land and fenced it in,
He cleared and ploughed the soil,
And year by year a richer crop
Repaid him for his toil.

Between the homes for many years
The devil left his tracks:
The squatter pounded Ross's stock,
And Sandy pounded Black's.
A well upon the lower run
Was filled with earth and logs,
And Black laid baits about the farm
To poison Ross's dogs.

It was, indeed, a deadly feud
Of class and creed and race;
But, yet, there was a Romeo
And a Juliet in the case;
And more than once across the flats,
Beneath the Southern Cross,
Young Robert Black was seen to ride
With pretty Jenny Ross.

One Christmas time, when months of drought
Had parched the western creeks,
The bush-fires started in the north
And travelled south for weeks.
At night along the river-side
The scene was grand and strange —
The hill-fires looked like lighted streets
Of cities in the range.

The cattle-tracks between the trees
Were like long dusky aisles,
And on a sudden breeze the fire
Would sweep along for miles;
Like sounds of distant musketry
It crackled through the brakes,
And o'er the flat of silver grass

It hissed like angry snakes.

It leapt across the flowing streams
And raced o'er pastures broad;
It climbed the trees and lit the boughs
And through the scrubs it roared.
The bees fell stifled in the smoke
Or perished in their hives,
And with the stock the kangaroos
Went flying for their lives.

The sun had set on Christmas Eve,
When, through the scrub-lands wide,
Young Robert Black came riding home
As only natives ride.
He galloped to the homestead door
And gave the first alarm:
'The fire is past the granite spur,
'And close to Ross's farm.'

'Now, father, send the men at once,
They won't be wanted here;
Poor Ross's wheat is all he has
To pull him through the year.'
'Then let it burn,' the squatter said;
'I'd like to see it done —
I'd bless the fire if it would clear
Selectors from the run.

'Go if you will,' the squatter said,
'You shall not take the men —
Go out and join your precious friends,
And don't come here again.'
'I won't come back,' young Robert cried,
And, reckless in his ire,
He sharply turned his horse's head
And galloped towards the fire.

And there, for three long weary hours,
Half-blind with smoke and heat,
Old Ross and Robert fought the flames
That neared the ripened wheat.
The farmer's hand was nerved by fears
Of danger and of loss;
And Robert fought the stubborn foe
For the love of Jenny Ross.

But serpent-like the curves and lines

Slipped past them, and between,
Until they reached the bound'ry where
The old coach-road had been.
'The track is now our only hope,
There we must stand,' cried Ross,
'For nought on earth can stop the fire
If once it gets across.'

Then came a cruel gust of wind,
And, with a fiendish rush,
The flames leapt o'er the narrow path
And lit the fence of brush.
'The crop must burn!' the farmer cried,
'We cannot save it now,'
And down upon the blackened ground
He dashed the ragged bough.

But wildly, in a rush of hope,
His heart began to beat,
For o'er the crackling fire he heard
The sound of horses' feet.
'Here's help at last,' young Robert cried,
And even as he spoke
The squatter with a dozen men
Came racing through the smoke.

Down on the ground the stockmen jumped
And bared each brawny arm,
They tore green branches from the trees
And fought for Ross's farm;
And when before the gallant band
The beaten flames gave way,
Two grimy hands in friendship joined —
And it was Christmas Day.

The Teams

A cloud of dust on the long white road,
And the teams go creeping on
Inch by inch with the weary load;
And by the power of the green-hide goad
The distant goal is won.

With eyes half-shut to the blinding dust,
And necks to the yokes bent low,
The beasts are pulling as bullocks must;

And the shining tires might almost rust
While the spokes are turning slow.

With face half-hid 'neath a broad-brimmed hat
That shades from the heat's white waves,
And shouldered whip with its green-hide plait,
The driver plods with a gait like that
Of his weary, patient slaves.

He wipes his brow, for the day is hot,
And spits to the left with spite;
He shouts at 'Bally', and flicks at 'Scot',
And raises dust from the back of 'Spot',
And spits to the dusty right.

He'll sometimes pause as a thing of form
In front of a settler's door,
And ask for a drink, and remark 'It's warm',
Or say 'There's signs of a thunder-storm';
But he seldom utters more.

But the rains are heavy on roads like these;
And, fronting his lonely home,
For weeks together the settler sees
The teams bogged down to the axletrees,
Or ploughing the sodden loam.

And then when the roads are at their worst,
The bushman's children hear
The cruel blows of the whips reversed
While bullocks pull as their hearts would burst,
And bellow with pain and fear.

And thus with little of joy or rest
Are the long, long journeys done;
And thus — 'tis a cruel war at the best —
Is distance fought in the mighty West,
And the lonely battles won.

Cameron's Heart

The diggings were just in their glory when Alister Cameron came,
With recommendations, he told me, from friends and a parson 'at hame';
He read me his recommendations — he called them a part of his plant —
The first one was signed by an Elder, the other by Cameron's aunt.
The meenister called him 'ungodly — a stray frae the fauld o' the Lord',

And his aunt set him down as a spendthrift, 'a rebel at hame and abroad'.

He got drunk now and then and he gambled (such heroes are often the same);
That's all they could say in connection with Alister Cameron's name.
He was straight and he stuck to his country and spoke with respect of his kirk;
He did his full share of the cooking, and more than his share of the work.
And many a poor devil then, when his strength and his money were spent,
Was sure of a lecture — and tucker, and a shakedown in Cameron's tent.

He shunned all the girls in the camp, and they said he was proof to the dart —
That nothing but whisky and gaming had ever a place in his heart;
He carried a packet about him, well hid, but I saw it at last,
And — well, 'tis a very old story — the story of Cameron's past:
A ring and a sprig o' white heather, a letter or two and a curl,
A bit of a worn silver chain, and the portrait of Cameron's girl.

It chanced in the first of the Sixties that Ally and I and McKean
Were sinking a shaft on Mundoorin, near Fosberry's puddle-machine.
The bucket we used was a big one, and rather a weight when 'twas full,
Though Alister wound it up easy, for he had the strength of a bull.
He hinted at heart-disease often, but, setting his fancy apart,
I always believed there was nothing the matter with Cameron's heart.

One day I was working below — I was filling the bucket with clay,
When Alister cried, 'Pack it on, mon! we ought to be bottomed to-day.'
He wound, and the bucket rose steady and swift to the surface until
It reached the first log on the top, where it suddenly stopped, and hung still.
I knew what was up in a moment when Cameron shouted to me:
'Climb up for your life by the footholes.
I'LL STICK TAE TH' HAUN'LE — OR DEE!'

And those were the last words he uttered.
He groaned, for I heard him quite plain —
There's nothing so awful as that when it's wrung from a workman in pain.
The strength of despair was upon me; I started, and scarcely drew breath,
But climbed to the top for my life in the fear of a terrible death.
And there, with his waist on the handle, I saw the dead form of my mate,
And over the shaft hung the bucket, suspended by Cameron's weight.

I wonder did Alister think of the scenes in the distance so dim,
When Death at the windlass that morning took cruel advantage of him?
He knew if the bucket rushed down it would murder or cripple his mate —
His hand on the iron was closed with a grip that was stronger than Fate;
He thought of my danger, not his, when he felt in his bosom the smart,
And stuck to the handle in spite of the Finger of Death on his heart.

The Shame of Going Back

When you've come to make a fortune and you haven't made your salt,
And the reason of your failure isn't anybody's fault —
When you haven't got a billet, and the times are very slack,
There is nothing that can spur you like the shame of going back;
Crawling home with empty pockets,
Going back hard-up;
Oh! it's then you learn the meaning of humiliation's cup.

When the place and you are strangers and you struggle all alone,
And you have a mighty longing for the town where you are known;
When your clothes are very shabby and the future's very black,
There is nothing that can hurt you like the shame of going back.

When we've fought the battle bravely and are beaten to the wall,
'Tis the sneers of men, not conscience, that make cowards of us all;
And the while you are returning, oh! your brain is on the rack,
And your heart is in the shadow of the shame of going back.

When a beaten man's discovered with a bullet in his brain,
They POST-MORTEM him, and try him, and they say he was insane;
But it very often happens that he'd lately got the sack,
And his onward move was owing to the shame of going back.

Ah! my friend, you call it nonsense, and your upper lip is curled,
I can see that you have never worked your passage through the world;
But when fortune rounds upon you and the rain is on the track,
You will learn the bitter meaning of the shame of going back;
Going home with empty pockets,
Going home hard-up;
Oh, you'll taste the bitter poison in humiliation's cup.

Since Then

I met Jack Ellis in town to-day —
Jack Ellis — my old mate, Jack —
Ten years ago, from the Castlereagh,
We carried our swags together away
To the Never-Again, Out Back.

But times have altered since those old days,
And the times have changed the men.
Ah, well! there's little to blame or praise —
Jack Ellis and I have tramped long ways
On different tracks since then.

His hat was battered, his coat was green,
The toes of his boots were through,
But the pride was his! It was I felt mean —
I wished that my collar was not so clean,
Nor the clothes I wore so new.

He saw me first, and he knew 'twas I —
The holiday swell he met.
Why have we no faith in each other? Ah, why? —
He made as though he would pass me by,
For he thought that I might forget.

He ought to have known me better than that,
By the tracks we tramped far out —
The sweltering scrub and the blazing flat,
When the heat came down through each old felt hat
In the hell-born western drought.

The cheques we made and the shanty sprees,
The camps in the great blind scrub,
The long wet tramps when the plains were seas,
And the oracles worked in days like these
For rum and tobacco and grub.

Could I forget how we struck 'the same
Old tale' in the nearer West,
When the first great test of our friendship came —
But — well, there's little to praise or blame
If our mateship stood the test.

'Heads!' he laughed (but his face was stern) —
'Tails!' and a friendly oath;
We loved her fair, we had much to learn —
And each was stabbed to the heart in turn
By the girl who — loved us both.

Or the last day lost on the lignum plain,
When I staggered, half-blind, half-dead,
With a burning throat and a tortured brain;
And the tank when we came to the track again
Was seventeen miles ahead.

Then life seemed finished — then death began
As down in the dust I sank,
But he stuck to his mate as a bushman can,
Till I heard him saying, 'Bear up, old man!'
In the shade by the mulga tank.

He took my hand in a distant way
(I thought how we parted last),
And we seemed like men who have nought to say
And who meet — 'Good-day', and who part — 'Good-day',
Who never have shared the past.

I asked him in for a drink with me —
Jack Ellis — my old mate, Jack —
But his manner no longer was careless and free,
He followed, but not with the grin that he
Wore always in days Out Back.

I tried to live in the past once more —
Or the present and past combine,
But the days between I could not ignore —
I couldn't help notice the clothes he wore,
And he couldn't but notice mine.

He placed his glass on the polished bar,
And he wouldn't fill up again;
For he is prouder than most men are —
Jack Ellis and I have tramped too far
On different tracks since then.

He said that he had a mate to meet,
And 'I'll see you again,' said he,
Then he hurried away through the crowded street
And the rattle of buses and scrape of feet
Seemed suddenly loud to me.

And I almost wished that the time were come
When less will be left to Fate —
When boys will start on the track from home
With equal chances, and no old chum
Have more or less than his mate.

Peter Anderson and Co.

He had offices in Sydney, not so many years ago,
And his shingle bore the legend 'Peter Anderson and Co.',
But his real name was Careless, as the fellows understood —
And his relatives decided that he wasn't any good.
'Twas their gentle tongues that blasted any 'character' he had —
He was fond of beer and leisure — and the Co. was just as bad.
It was limited in number to a unit, was the Co. —

'Twas a bosom chum of Peter and his Christian name was Joe.

'Tis a class of men belonging to these soul-forsaken years:
Third-rate canvassers, collectors, journalists and auctioneers.
They are never very shabby, they are never very spruce —
Going cheerfully and carelessly and smoothly to the deuce.
Some are wanderers by profession, 'turning up' and gone as soon,
Travelling second-class, or steerage (when it's cheap they go saloon);
Free from 'ists' and 'isms', troubled little by belief or doubt —
Lazy, purposeless, and useless — knocking round and hanging out.
They will take what they can get, and they will give what they can give,
God alone knows how they manage — God alone knows how they live!
They are nearly always hard-up, but are cheerful all the while —
Men whose energy and trousers wear out sooner than their smile!
They, no doubt, like us, are haunted by the boresome 'if' or 'might',
But their ghosts are ghosts of daylight — they are men who live at night!

Peter met you with the comic smile of one who knows you well,
And is mighty glad to see you, and has got a joke to tell;
He could laugh when all was gloomy, he could grin when all was blue,
Sing a comic song and act it, and appreciate it, too.
Only cynical in cases where his own self was the jest,
And the humour of his good yarns made atonement for the rest.
Seldom serious — doing business just as 'twere a friendly game —
Cards or billiards — nothing graver. And the Co. was much the same.

They tried everything and nothing 'twixt the shovel and the press,
And were more or less successful in their ventures — mostly less.
Once they ran a country paper till the plant was seized for debt,
And the local sinners chuckle over dingy copies yet.

They'd been through it all and knew it in the land of Bills and Jims —
Using Peter's own expression, they had been in 'various swims'.
Now and then they'd take an office, as they called it, — make a dash
Into business life as 'agents' — something not requiring cash.
(You can always furnish cheaply, when your cash or credit fails,
With a packing-case, a hammer, and a pound of two-inch nails —
And, maybe, a drop of varnish and sienna, too, for tints,
And a scrap or two of oilcloth, and a yard or two of chintz).
They would pull themselves together, pay a week's rent in advance,
But it never lasted longer than a month by any chance.

The office was their haven, for they lived there when hard-up —
A 'daily' for a table cloth — a jam tin for a cup;
And if the landlord's bailiff happened round in times like these
And seized the office-fittings — well, there wasn't much to seize —
They would leave him in possession. But at other times they shot
The moon, and took an office where the landlord knew them not.

And when morning brought the bailiff there'd be nothing to be seen
Save a piece of bevelled cedar where the tenant's plate had been;
There would be no sign of Peter — there would be no sign of Joe
Till another portal boasted 'Peter Anderson and Co.'

And when times were locomotive, billiard-rooms and private bars —
Spicy parties at the cafe — long cab-drives beneath the stars;
Private picnics down the Harbour — shady campings-out, you know —
No one would have dreamed 'twas Peter —
no one would have thought 'twas Joe!
Free-and-easies in their 'diggings', when the funds began to fail,
Bosom chums, cigars, tobacco, and a case of English ale —
Gloriously drunk and happy, till they heard the roosters crow —
And the landlady and neighbours made complaints about the Co.
But that life! it might be likened to a reckless drinking-song,
For it can't go on for ever, and it never lasted long.

Debt-collecting ruined Peter — people talked him round too oft,
For his heart was soft as butter (and the Co.'s was just as soft);
He would cheer the haggard missus, and he'd tell her not to fret,
And he'd ask the worried debtor round with him to have a wet;
He would ask him round the corner, and it seemed to him and her,
After each of Peter's visits, things were brighter than they were.
But, of course, it wasn't business — only Peter's careless way;
And perhaps it pays in heaven, but on earth it doesn't pay.
They got harder up than ever, and, to make it worse, the Co.
Went more often round the corner than was good for him to go.

'I might live,' he said to Peter, 'but I haven't got the nerve —
I am going, Peter, going — going, going — no reserve.
Eat and drink and love they tell us, for to-morrow we may die,
Buy experience — and we bought it — we're experienced, you and I.'
Then, with a weary movement of his hand across his brow:
'The death of such philosophy's the death I'm dying now.
Pull yourself together, Peter; 'tis the dying wish of Joe
That the business world shall honour Peter Anderson and Co.

'When you feel your life is sinking in a dull and useless course,
And begin to find in drinking keener pleasure and remorse —
When you feel the love of leisure on your careless heart take holt,
Break away from friends and pleasure, though it give your heart a jolt.
Shun the poison breath of cities — billiard-rooms and private bars,
Go where you can breathe God's air and see the grandeur of the stars!
Find again and follow up the old ambitions that you had —
See if you can raise a drink, old man, I'm feelin' mighty bad —
Hot and sweetened, nip o' butter — squeeze o' lemon, Pete,' he sighed.
And, while Peter went to fetch it, Joseph went to sleep — and died
With a smile — anticipation, maybe, of the peace to come,

Or a joke to try on Peter — or, perhaps, it was the rum.

Peter staggered, gripped the table, swerved as some old drunkard swerves —
At a gulp he drank the toddy, just to brace his shattered nerves.
It was awful, if you like. But then he hadn't time to think —
All is nothing! Nothing matters! Fill your glasses — dead man's drink.

Yet, to show his heart was not of human decency bereft,
Peter paid the undertaker. He got drunk on what was left;
Then he shed some tears, half-maudlin, on the grave where lay the Co.,
And he drifted to a township where the city failures go.
Where, though haunted by the man he was, the wreck he yet might be,
Or the man he might have been, or by each spectre of the three,
And the dying words of Joseph, ringing through his own despair,
Peter 'pulled himself together' and he started business there.

But his life was very lonely, and his heart was very sad,
And no help to reformation was the company he had —
Men who might have been, who had been, but who were not in the swim —
'Twas a town of wrecks and failures — they appreciated him.
They would ask him who the Co. was — that queer company he kept —
And he'd always answer vaguely — he would say his partner slept;
That he had a 'sleeping partner' — jesting while his spirit broke —
And they grinned above their glasses, for they took it as a joke.
He would shout while he had money, he would joke while he had breath —
No one seemed to care or notice how he drank himself to death;
Till at last there came a morning when his smile was seen no more —
He was gone from out the office, and his shingle from the door,
And a boundary-rider jogging out across the neighb'ring run
Was attracted by a something that was blazing in the sun;
And he found that it was Peter, lying peacefully at rest,
With a bottle close beside him and the shingle on his breast.
Well, they analysed the liquor, and it would appear that he
Qualified his drink with something good for setting spirits free.
Though 'twas plainly self-destruction — "twas his own affair,' they said;
And the jury viewed him sadly, and they found — that he was dead.

When the Children Come Home

On a lonely selection far out in the West
An old woman works all the day without rest,
And she croons, as she toils 'neath the sky's glassy dome,
'Sure I'll keep the ould place till the childer come home.'

She mends all the fences, she grubs, and she ploughs,
She drives the old horse and she milks all the cows,

And she sings to herself as she thatches the stack,
'Sure I'll keep the ould place till the childer come back.'

It is five weary years since her old husband died;
And oft as he lay on his deathbed he sighed
'Sure one man can bring up ten children, he can,
An' it's strange that ten sons cannot keep one old man.'

Whenever the scowling old sundowners come,
And cunningly ask if the master's at home,
'Be off,' she replies, 'with your blarney and cant,
Or I'll call my son Andy; he's workin' beyant.'

'Git out,' she replies, though she trembles with fear,
For she lives all alone and no neighbours are near;
But she says to herself, when she's like to despond,
That the boys are at work in the paddock beyond.

Ah, none of her children need follow the plough,
And some have grown rich in the city ere now;
Yet she says: 'They might come when the shearing is done,
And I'll keep the ould place if it's only for one.'

Dan, the Wreck

Tall, and stout, and solid-looking,
Yet a wreck;
None would think Death's finger's hooking
Him from deck.
Cause of half the fun that's started —
'Hard-case' Dan —
Isn't like a broken-hearted,
Ruined man.

Walking-coat from tail to throat is
Frayed and greened —
Like a man whose other coat is
Being cleaned;
Gone for ever round the edging
Past repair —
Waistcoat pockets frayed with dredging
After 'sprats' no longer there.

Wearing summer boots in June, or
Slippers worn and old —
Like a man whose other shoon are

Getting soled.
Pants? They're far from being recent —
But, perhaps, I'd better not —
Says they are the only decent
Pair he's got.

And his hat, I am afraid, is
Troubling him —
Past all lifting to the ladies
By the brim.
But, although he'd hardly strike a
Girl, would Dan,
Yet he wears his wreckage like a
Gentleman!

Once — no matter how the rest dressed —
Up or down —
Once, they say, he was the best-dressed
Man in town.
Must have been before I knew him —
Now you'd scarcely care to meet
And be noticed talking to him
In the street.

Drink the cause, and dissipation,
That is clear —
Maybe friend or kind relation
Cause of beer.
And the talking fool, who never
Reads or thinks,
Says, from hearsay: 'Yes, he's clever;
But, you know, he drinks.'

Been an actor and a writer —
Doesn't whine —
Reckoned now the best reciter
In his line.
Takes the stage at times, and fills it —
'Princess May' or 'Waterloo'.
Raise a sneer! — his first line kills it,
'Brings 'em', too.

Where he lives, or how, or wherefore
No one knows;
Lost his real friends, and therefore
Lost his foes.
Had, no doubt, his own romances —
Met his fate;

Tortured, doubtless, by the chances
And the luck that comes too late.

Now and then his boots are polished,
Collar clean,
And the worst grease stains abolished
By ammonia or benzine:
Hints of some attempt to shove him
From the taps,
Or of someone left to love him —
Sister, p'r'aps.

After all, he is a grafter,
Earns his cheer —
Keeps the room in roars of laughter
When he gets outside a beer.
Yarns that would fall flat from others
He can tell;
How he spent his 'stuff', my brothers,
You know well.

Manner puts a man in mind of
Old club balls and evening dress,
Ugly with a handsome kind of
Ugliness.

One of those we say of often,
While hearts swell,
Standing sadly by the coffin:
'He looks well.'

We may be — so goes a rumour —
Bad as Dan;
But we may not have the humour
Of the man;
Nor the sight — well, deem it blindness,
As the general public do —
And the love of human kindness,
Or the GRIT to see it through!

A Prouder Man Than You

If you fancy that your people came of better stock than mine,
If you hint of higher breeding by a word or by a sign,
If you're proud because of fortune or the clever things you do —
Then I'll play no second fiddle: I'm a prouder man than you!

If you think that your profession has the more gentility,
And that you are condescending to be seen along with me;
If you notice that I'm shabby while your clothes are spruce and new —
You have only got to hint it: I'm a prouder man than you!

If you have a swell companion when you see me on the street,
And you think that I'm too common for your toney friend to meet,
So that I, in passing closely, fail to come within your view —
Then be blind to me for ever: I'm a prouder man than you!

If your character be blameless, if your outward past be clean,
While 'tis known my antecedents are not what they should have been,
Do not risk contamination, save your name whate'er you do —
'Birds o' feather fly together': I'm a prouder bird than you!

Keep your patronage for others! Gold and station cannot hide
Friendship that can laugh at fortune, friendship that can conquer pride!
Offer this as to an equal — let me see that you are true,
And my wall of pride is shattered: I am not so proud as you!

The Song and the Sigh

The creek went down with a broken song,
'Neath the sheoaks high;
The waters carried the song along,
And the oaks a sigh.

The song and the sigh went winding by,
Went winding down;
Circling the foot of the mountain high,
And the hillside brown.

They were hushed in the swamp of the Dead Man's Crime,
Where the curlews cried;
But they reached the river the self-same time,
And there they died.

And the creek of life goes winding on,
Wandering by;
And bears for ever, its course upon,
A song and a sigh.

The Cambaroora Star

So you're writing for a paper? Well, it's nothing very new
To be writing yards of drivel for a tidy little screw;
You are young and educated, and a clever chap you are,
But you'll never run a paper like the CAMBAROORA STAR.
Though in point of education I am nothing but a dunce,
I myself — you mayn't believe it — helped to run a paper once
With a chap on Cambaroora, by the name of Charlie Brown,
And I'll tell you all about it if you'll take the story down.

On a golden day in summer, when the sunrays were aslant,
Brown arrived in Cambaroora with a little printing plant
And his worldly goods and chattels — rather damaged on the way —
And a weary-looking woman who was following the dray.
He had bought an empty humpy, and, instead of getting tight,
Why, the diggers heard him working like a lunatic all night:
And next day a sign of canvas, writ in characters of tar,
Claimed the humpy as the office of the CAMBAROORA STAR.

Well, I cannot read, that's honest, but I had a digger friend
Who would read the paper to me from the title to the end;
And the STAR contained a leader running thieves and spielers down,
With a slap against claim-jumping, and a poem made by Brown.
Once I showed it to a critic, and he said 'twas very fine,
Though he wasn't long in finding glaring faults in every line;
But it was a song of Freedom — all the clever critic said
Couldn't stop that song from ringing, ringing, ringing in my head.

So I went where Brown was working in his little hut hard by:
'My old mate has been a-reading of your writings, Brown,' said I —
'I have studied on your leader, I agree with what you say,
You have struck the bed-rock certain, and there ain't no get-away;
Your paper's just the thumper for a young and growing land,
And your principles is honest, Brown; I want to shake your hand,
And if there's any lumping in connection with the STAR,
Well, I'll find the time to do it, and I'll help you — there you are!'

Brown was every inch a digger (bronzed and bearded in the South),
But there seemed a kind of weakness round the corners of his mouth
When he took the hand I gave him; and he gripped it like a vice,
While he tried his best to thank me, and he stuttered once or twice.
But there wasn't need for talking — we'd the same old loves and hates,
And we understood each other — Charlie Brown and I were mates.
So we worked a little 'paddock' on a place they called the 'Bar',
And we sank a shaft together, and at night we worked the STAR.

Charlie thought and did his writing when his work was done at night,
And the missus used to 'set' it near as quick as he could write.

Well, I didn't shirk my promise, and I helped the thing, I guess,
For at night I worked the lever of the crazy printing-press;
Brown himself would do the feeding, and the missus used to 'fly' —
She is flying with the angels, if there's justice up on high,
For she died on Cambaroora when the STAR began to go,
And was buried like the diggers buried diggers long ago.

Lord, that press! It was a jumper — we could seldom get it right,
And were lucky if we averaged a hundred in the night.
Many nights we'd sit together in the windy hut and fold,
And I helped the thing a little when I struck a patch of gold;
And we battled for the diggers as the papers seldom do,
Though when the diggers errored, why, we touched the diggers too.
Yet the paper took the fancy of that roaring mining town,
And the diggers sent a nugget with their sympathy to Brown.

Oft I sat and smoked beside him in the listening hours of night,
When the shadows from the corners seemed to gather round the light —
When his weary, aching fingers, closing stiffly round the pen,
Wrote defiant truth in language that could touch the hearts of men —
Wrote until his eyelids shuddered — wrote until the East was grey:
Wrote the stern and awful lessons that were taught him in his day;
And they knew that he was honest, and they read his smallest par,
For I think the diggers' Bible was the CAMBAROORA STAR.

Diggers then had little mercy for the loafer and the scamp —
If there wasn't law and order, there was justice in the camp;
And the manly independence that is found where diggers are
Had a sentinel to guard it in the CAMBAROORA STAR.
There was strife about the Chinamen, who came in days of old
Like a swarm of thieves and loafers when the diggers found the gold —
Like the sneaking fortune-hunters who are always found behind,
And who only shepherd diggers till they track them to the 'find'.

Charlie wrote a slinging leader, calling on his digger mates,
And he said: 'We think that Chinkies are as bad as syndicates.
What's the good of holding meetings where you only talk and swear?
Get a move upon the Chinkies when you've got an hour to spare.'
It was nine o'clock next morning when the Chows began to swarm,
But they weren't so long in going, for the diggers' blood was warm.
Then the diggers held a meeting, and they shouted: 'Hip hoorar!
Give three ringing cheers, my hearties, for the CAMBAROORA STAR.'

But the Cambaroora petered, and the diggers' sun went down,
And another sort of people came and settled in the town;
The reefing was conducted by a syndicate or two,
And they changed the name to 'Queensville', for their blood was very blue.
They wanted Brown to help them put the feathers in their nests,

But his leaders went like thunder for their vested interests,
And he fought for right and justice and he raved about the dawn
Of the reign of Man and Reason till his ads. were all withdrawn.

He was offered shares for nothing in the richest of the mines,
And he could have made a fortune had he run on other lines;
They abused him for his leaders, and they parodied his rhymes,
And they told him that his paper was a mile behind the times.
'Let the times alone,' said Charlie, 'they're all right, you needn't fret;
For I started long before them, and they haven't caught me yet.
But,' says he to me, 'they're coming, and they're not so very far —
Though I left the times behind me they are following the STAR.

'Let them do their worst,' said Charlie, 'but I'll never drop the reins
While a single scrap of paper or an ounce of ink remains:
I've another truth to tell them, though they tread me in the dirt,
And I'll print another issue if I print it on my shirt.'
So we fought the battle bravely, and we did our very best
Just to make the final issue quite as lively as the rest.
And the swells in Cambaroora talked of feathers and of tar
When they read the final issue of the CAMBAROORA STAR.

Gold is stronger than the tongue is — gold is stronger than the pen:
They'd have squirmed in Cambaroora had I found a nugget then;
But in vain we scraped together every penny we could get,
For they fixed us with their boycott, and the plant was seized for debt.
'Twas a storekeeper who did it, and he sealed the paper's doom,
Though we gave him ads. for nothing when the STAR began to boom:
'Twas a paltry bill for tucker, and the crawling, sneaking clown
Sold the debt for twice its value to the men who hated Brown.

I was digging up the river, and I swam the flooded bend
With a little cash and comfort for my literary friend.
Brown was sitting sad and lonely with his head bowed in despair,
While a single tallow candle threw a flicker on his hair,
And the gusty wind that whistled through the crannies of the door
Stirred the scattered files of paper that were lying on the floor.
Charlie took my hand in silence — and by-and-by he said:
'Tom, old mate, we did our damnedest, but the brave old STAR is dead.'

Then he stood up on a sudden, with a face as pale as death,
And he gripped my hand a moment, while he seemed to fight for breath:
'Tom, old friend,' he said, 'I'm going, and I'm ready to — to start,
For I know that there is something — something crooked with my heart.
Tom, my first child died. I loved her even better than the pen —
Tom — and while the STAR was dying, why, I felt like I did THEN.

Listen! Like the distant thunder of the rollers on the bar —
Listen, Tom! I hear the — diggers — shouting: 'Bully for the STAR!"

After All

The brooding ghosts of Australian night have gone from the bush and town;
My spirit revives in the morning breeze, though it died when the sun went down;
The river is high and the stream is strong, and the grass is green and tall,
And I fain would think that this world of ours is a good world after all.

The light of passion in dreamy eyes, and a page of truth well read,
The glorious thrill in a heart grown cold of the spirit I thought was dead,
A song that goes to a comrade's heart, and a tear of pride let fall —
And my soul is strong! and the world to me is a grand world after all!

Let our enemies go by their old dull tracks, and theirs be the fault or shame
(The man is bitter against the world who has only himself to blame);
Let the darkest side of the past be dark, and only the good recall;
For I must believe that the world, my dear, is a kind world after all.

It well may be that I saw too plain, and it may be I was blind;
But I'll keep my face to the dawning light, though the devil may stand behind!
Though the devil may stand behind my back, I'll not see his shadow fall,
But read the signs in the morning stars of a good world after all.

Rest, for your eyes are weary, girl — you have driven the worst away —
The ghost of the man that I might have been is gone from my heart to-day;
We'll live for life and the best it brings till our twilight shadows fall;
My heart grows brave, and the world, my girl, is a good world after all.

Marshall's Mate

You almost heard the surface bake, and saw the gum-leaves turn —
You could have watched the grass scorch brown had there been grass to burn.
In such a drought the strongest heart might well grow faint and weak —
'Twould frighten Satan to his home — not far from Dingo Creek.

The tanks went dry on Ninety Mile, as tanks go dry out back,
The Half-Way Spring had failed at last when Marshall missed the track;
Beneath a dead tree on the plain we saw a pack-horse reel —
Too blind to see there was no shade, and too done-up to feel.
And charcoaled on the canvas bag ('twas written pretty clear)
We read the message Marshall wrote. It said: 'I'm taken queer —
I'm somewhere off of Deadman's Track, half-blind and nearly dead;

Find Crowbar, get him sobered up, and follow back,' it said.

'Let Mitchell go to Bandicoot. You'll find him there,' said Mack.
'I'll start the chaps from Starving Steers, and take the dry-holes back.'
We tramped till dark, and tried to track the pack-horse on the sands,
And just at daylight Crowbar came with Milroy's station hands.
His cheeks were drawn, his face was white, but he was sober then —
In times of trouble, fire, and flood, 'twas Crowbar led the men.
'Spread out as widely as you can each side the track,' said he;
'The first to find him make a smoke that all the rest can see.'

We took the track and followed back where Crowbar followed fate,
We found a dead man in the scrub — but 'twas not Crowbar's mate.
The station hands from Starving Steers were searching all the week —
But never news of Marshall's fate came back to Dingo Creek.
And no one, save the spirit of the sand-waste, fierce and lone,
Knew where Jack Marshall crawled to die — but Crowbar might have known.

He'd scarcely closed his quiet eyes or drawn a sleeping breath —
They say that Crowbar slept no more until he slept in death.
A careless, roving scamp, that loved to laugh and drink and joke,
But no man saw him smile again (and no one saw him smoke),
And, when we spelled at night, he'd lie with eyes still open wide,
And watch the stars as if they'd point the place where Marshall died.

The search was made as searches are (and often made in vain),
And on the seventh day we saw a smoke across the plain;
We left the track and followed back — 'twas Crowbar still that led,
And when his horse gave out at last he walked and ran ahead.
We reached the place and turned again — dragged back and no man spoke —
It was a bush-fire in the scrubs that made the cursed smoke.
And when we gave it best at last, he said, 'I'LL see it through,'
Although he knew we'd done as much as mortal men could do.
'I'll not — I won't give up!' he said, his hand pressed to his brow;
'My God! the cursed flies and ants, they might be at him now.
I'll see it so in twenty years, 'twill haunt me all my life —
I could not face his sister, and I could not face his wife.
It's no use talking to me now — I'm going back,' he said,
'I'm going back to find him, and I will — alive or dead!'

He packed his horse with water and provisions for a week,
And then, at sunset, crossed the plain, away from Dingo Creek.
We watched him tramp beside the horse till we, as it grew late,
Could not tell which was Bonypart and which was Marshall's mate.
The dam went dry at Dingo Creek, and we were driven back,
And none dared face the Ninety Mile when Crowbar took the track.

They saw him at Dead Camel and along the Dry Hole Creeks —

There came a day when none had heard of Marshall's mate for weeks;
They'd seen him at No Sunday, he called at Starving Steers —
There came a time when none had heard of Marshall's mate for years.
They found old Bonypart at last, picked clean by hungry crows,
But no one knew how Crowbar died — the soul of Marshall knows!

And now, way out on Dingo Creek, when winter days are late,
The bushmen talk of Crowbar's ghost 'what's looking for his mate';
For let the fools indulge their mirth, and let the wise men doubt —
The soul of Crowbar and his mate have travelled further out.
Beyond the furthest two-rail fence, Colanne and Nevertire —
Beyond the furthest rabbit-proof, barbed wire and common wire —
Beyond the furthest 'Gov'ment' tank, and past the furthest bore —
The Never-Never, No Man's Land, No More, and Nevermore —
Beyond the Land o' Break-o'-Day, and Sunset and the Dawn,
The soul of Marshall and the soul of Marshall's mate have gone
Unto that Loving, Laughing Land where life is fresh and clean —
Where the rivers flow all summer, and the grass is always green.

The Poets of the Tomb

The world has had enough of bards who wish that they were dead,
'Tis time the people passed a law to knock 'em on the head,
For 'twould be lovely if their friends could grant the rest they crave —
Those bards of 'tears' and 'vanished hopes', those poets of the grave.
They say that life's an awful thing, and full of care and gloom,
They talk of peace and restfulness connected with the tomb.

They say that man is made of dirt, and die, of course, he must;
But, all the same, a man is made of pretty solid dust.
There is a thing that they forget, so let it here be writ,
That some are made of common mud, and some are made of GRIT;
Some try to help the world along while others fret and fume
And wish that they were slumbering in the silence of the tomb.

'Twixt mother's arms and coffin-gear a man has work to do!
And if he does his very best he mostly worries through,
And while there is a wrong to right, and while the world goes round,
An honest man alive is worth a million underground.
And yet, as long as sheoaks sigh and wattle-blossoms bloom,
The world shall hear the drivel of the poets of the tomb.

And though the graveyard poets long to vanish from the scene,
I notice that they mostly wish their resting-place kept green.
Now, were I rotting underground, I do not think I'd care
If wombats rooted on the mound or if the cows camped there;

And should I have some feelings left when I have gone before,
I think a ton of solid stone would hurt my feelings more.

Such wormy songs of mouldy joys can give me no delight;
I'll take my chances with the world, I'd rather live and fight.
Though Fortune laughs along my track, or wears her blackest frown,
I'll try to do the world some good before I tumble down.
Let's fight for things that ought to be, and try to make 'em boom;
We cannot help mankind when we are ashes in the tomb.

Australian Bards and Bush Reviewers

While you use your best endeavour to immortalise in verse
The gambling and the drink which are your country's greatest curse,
While you glorify the bully and take the spieler's part —
You're a clever southern writer, scarce inferior to Bret Harte.

If you sing of waving grasses when the plains are dry as bricks,
And discover shining rivers where there's only mud and sticks;
If you picture 'mighty forests' where the mulga spoils the view —
You're superior to Kendall, and ahead of Gordon too.

If you swear there's not a country like the land that gave you birth,
And its sons are just the noblest and most glorious chaps on earth;
If in every girl a Venus your poetic eye discerns,
You are gracefully referred to as the 'young Australian Burns'.

But if you should find that bushmen — spite of all the poets say —
Are just common brother-sinners, and you're quite as good as they —
You're a drunkard, and a liar, and a cynic, and a sneak,
Your grammar's simply awful and your intellect is weak.

The Ghost

Down the street as I was drifting with the city's human tide,
Came a ghost, and for a moment walked in silence by my side —
Now my heart was hard and bitter, and a bitter spirit he,
So I felt no great aversion to his ghostly company.
Said the Shade: 'At finer feelings let your lip in scorn be curled,
'Self and Pelf', my friend, has ever been the motto for the world.'

And he said: 'If you'd be happy, you must clip your fancy's wings,
Stretch your conscience at the edges to the size of earthly things;
Never fight another's battle, for a friend can never know

When he'll gladly fly for succour to the bosom of the foe.
At the power of truth and friendship let your lip in scorn be curled —
'Self and Pelf', my friend, remember, is the motto of the world.

'Where Society is mighty, always truckle to her rule;
Never send an 'i' undotted to the teacher of a school;
Only fight a wrong or falsehood when the crowd is at your back,
And, till Charity repay you, shut the purse, and let her pack;
At the fools who would do other let your lip in scorn be curled,
'Self and Pelf', my friend, remember, that's the motto of the world.

'Ne'er assail the shaky ladders Fame has from her niches hung,
Lest unfriendly heels above you grind your fingers from the rung;
Or the fools who idle under, envious of your fair renown,
Heedless of the pain you suffer, do their worst to shake you down.
At the praise of men, or censure, let your lip in scorn be curled,
'Self and Pelf', my friend, remember, is the motto of the world.

'Flowing founts of inspiration leave their sources parched and dry,
Scalding tears of indignation sear the hearts that beat too high;
Chilly waters thrown upon it drown the fire that's in the bard;
And the banter of the critic hurts his heart till it grows hard.
At the fame your muse may offer let your lip in scorn be curled,
'Self and Pelf', my friend, remember, that's the motto of the world.

'Shun the fields of love, where lightly, to a low and mocking tune,
Strong and useful lives are ruined, and the broken hearts are strewn.
Not a farthing is the value of the honest love you hold;
Call it lust, and make it serve you! Set your heart on nought but gold.
At the bliss of purer passions let your lip in scorn be curled —
'Self and Pelf', my friend, shall ever be the motto of the world.'

Then he ceased and looked intently in my face, and nearer drew;
But a sudden deep repugnance to his presence thrilled me through;
Then I saw his face was cruel, by the look that o'er it stole,
Then I felt his breath was poison, by the shuddering of my soul,
Then I guessed his purpose evil, by his lip in sneering curled,
And I knew he slandered mankind, by my knowledge of the world.

But he vanished as a purer brighter presence gained my side —
'Heed him not! there's truth and friendship in this wondrous world,' she cried,
And of those who cleave to virtue in their climbing for renown,
Only they who faint or falter from the height are shaken down.
At a cynic's baneful teaching let your lip in scorn be curled!
'Brotherhood and Love and Honour!' is the motto for the world.'

Henry Archibald Hertzberg Lawson was born on the 17th June 1867 in a town on the Grenfell goldfields of New South Wales, Australia.

His parents, father Niel, a Norwegian born miner and mother Louisa, a noted poet, publisher and feminist were married on 7th July 1866 when he was 32 and she 18. On Henry's birth, the family surname was Anglicised to Lawson. The couple were to have an unhappy marriage despite producing three children.

Lawson attended school at Eurunderee from October 1876 but an ear infection he contracted left him partially deaf. By fourteen he had lost his hearing completely.

Lawson later attended a Catholic school at Mudgee, New South Wales where he developed an interest in poetry and, on his mother's influence, immersed himself in books given that learning in the classroom, with his deafness, was a major hurdle.

In 1883, after working on construction jobs with his father in the Blue Mountains, Lawson joined his mother in Sydney where she was living with his siblings. Here, Lawson worked during the day and studied at night for his matriculation in the hopes of enrolling at university. However, he failed his exams.

His first published poem was 'A Song of the Republic' in The Bulletin on 1st October 1887. This was quickly followed by other published poems with one recognising him as "a youth whose poetic genius here speaks eloquently for itself."

In 1890 he began a relationship with Mary Gilmore but it broke down due to his frequent absences from Sydney.

Lawson received an offer to write for the Brisbane Boomerang in 1891, but financial troubles at the magazine made this a short stint of only a few months. Despite writing for other magazines in Brisbane it was a dead end.

He returned to Sydney and continued to write for the Bulletin which, in 1892, engaged him for an inland trip where he could write articles about the harsh realities of life in drought-stricken New South Wales. He also took some time to work as a roustabout (an unskilled or semi-skilled worker) in the woolshed at Toorale Station. This resulted in his contributions to the Bulletin Debate and became the experience he used for a number of his stories in subsequent years. For Lawson this was an eye-opening period. His grim view of the outback was far removed from the romantic idyll of bravery and beauty inked in the poetry of his contemporary Banjo Paterson.

In 1896, Lawson married Bertha Bredt, Jr., daughter of Bertha Bredt, the prominent socialist. The marriage ended very unhappily in June 1903. They had two children.

Despite this Lawson was finding his way in the literary world. His writing was achieving recognition. His most successful prose collection 'While the Billy Boils', was published in 1896. In it he virtually reinvented Australian realism.

His writing style of short, sharp sentences with honed and sparse descriptions created a personal writing style that defined Australians: dryly laconic, passionately egalitarian and deeply humane. Most of Lawson's work centres on the Australian bush, it's fabled outback, such as in the desolate 'Past Carin', and is considered by many to vividly portray the real Australian life at that time.

Like the majority of Australians, Lawson lived in a city, but had had plenty of experience in outback life, these two outlooks helped shape a very individual talent. Unfortunately, his life was also flawed with other issues.

In Sydney in 1898 he was a prominent member of the Dawn and Dusk Club, a bohemian club of writer friends who met for drinks and conversation.

Sadly, for Lawson despite his growing recognition and fame he became withdrawn and unable to take part in the usual routines of life. His struggles with alcohol and mental health issues continued to drain him. His once prolific literary output began to decline. At times he was destitute mainly due, despite good sales and an enthusiastic audience, to ruinous publishing deals he had entered into.

In 1903 he bought a room at Mrs Isabel Byers' Coffee Palace in North Sydney. This near 20-year friendship between Mrs Byers and Lawson was a bedrock for him. Despite his position as the most celebrated Australian writer of the time, Lawson was deeply depressed and perpetually poor. His ex-wife repeatedly reported him for non-payment of child maintenance, which resulted in numerous jail terms or periods in psychiatric institutions. He was incarcerated at Darlinghurst Gaol for drunkenness, wife desertion, child desertion, and non-payment of child support seven times between 1905 and 1909 and spent a total of 159 days in prison. He wrote about these experiences in the haunting poem 'One Hundred and Three'—his prison number—which was published in 1908.

Mrs Byers was a good poet herself and, although of modest education, had been writing vivid poetry since her teens in a somewhat similar style to Lawson's. Long separated from her husband and elderly, Mrs Byers was, at the time she met Lawson, a woman of independent means looking forward to a comfortable retirement. She regarded Lawson as Australia's greatest living poet, and hoped to sustain him well enough to keep him writing. She acted as his agent in negotiations with publishers, helped to arrange contact with his children, contacted friends and supporters to help him financially, as well as assisting and nursing him through his mental health issues and problems with alcohol. She wrote countless letters on his behalf and pursued any avenue that could provide Lawson with financial support or a publishing deal.

Regardless of all else Lawson was a vocal nationalist and republican and took pride that many of his works were helping to establish the Australian vernacular in fiction.

Henry Archibald Hertzberg Lawson died, of a cerebral hemorrhage, in Mrs Byer's home in Abbotsford, Sydney on 2nd September 1922.

Lawson became the first Australian writer to be granted a state funeral. It was attended by the Prime Minister Billy Hughes and the (later) Premier of New South Wales, Jack Lang (the husband of Lawson's sister-in-law Hilda Bredt), as well as thousands of citizens.

Henry Lawson – A Concise Bibliography

Short Stories in Prose and Verse (1894)
While the Billy Boils (1896)
In the Days When the World was Wide and Other Verses (1896)
Verses, Popular and Humorous (1900)
On the Track (1900)
Over the Sliprails (1900)
On the Track, and, Over the Sliprails (1900)
Popular Verses (1900)
Humorous Verses (1900)
The Country I Come From (1901)
Joe Wilson and His Mates (1901)
Children of the Bush (1902)
When I Was King and Other Verses (1905)
The Elder Son (1905)
When I Was King (1905)
The Romance of the Swag (1907)
Send Round the Hat (1907)
The Skyline Riders and Other Verses (1910)
The Rising of the Court and Other Sketches in Prose and Verse (1910)
For Australia and Other Poems (1913)
Triangles of Life and Other Stories (1913)
My Army, O, My Army! and Other Songs (1915)
Song of the Dardanelles and Other Verses (1916)
Selected Poems of Henry Lawson (1918)